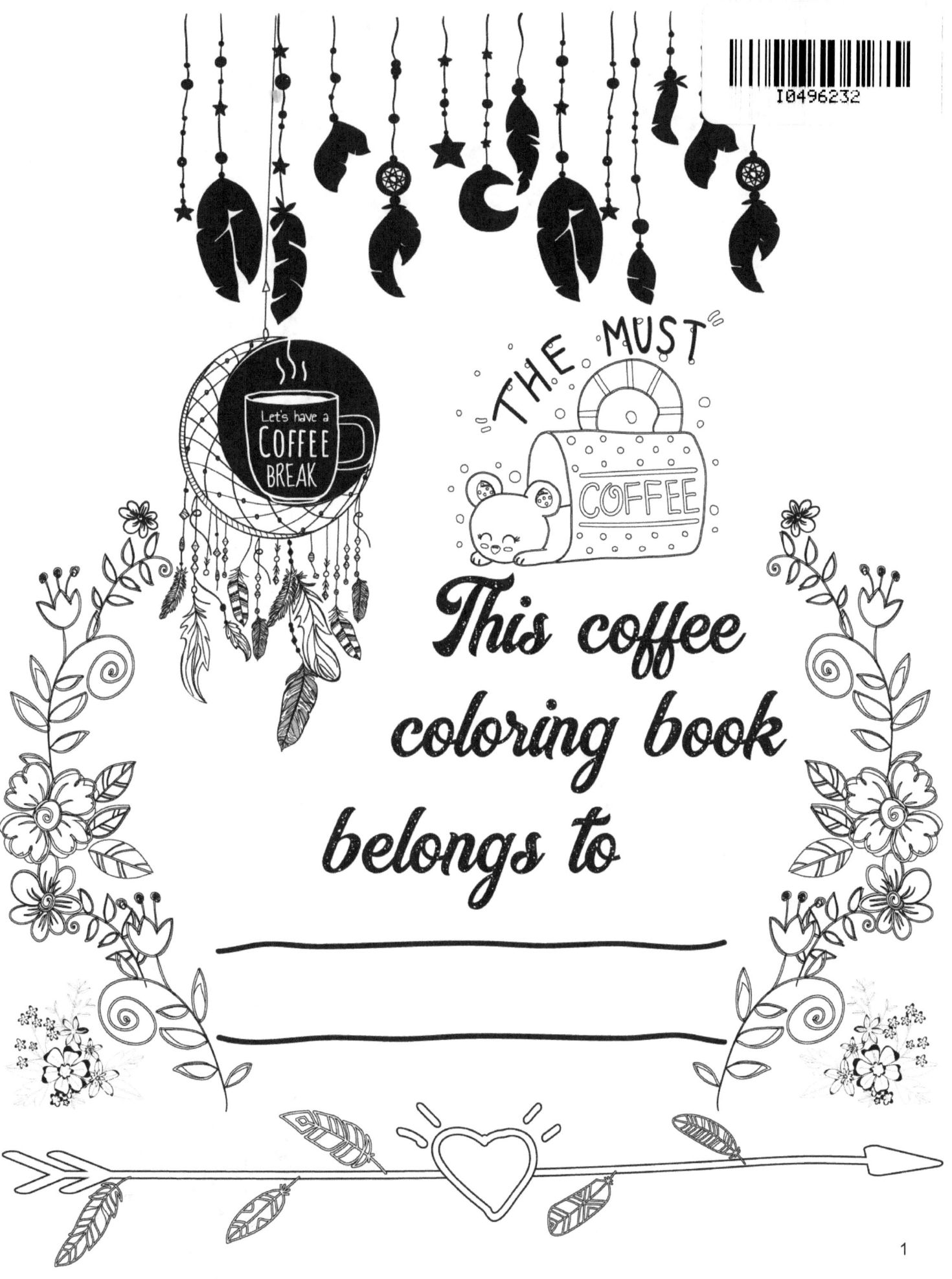

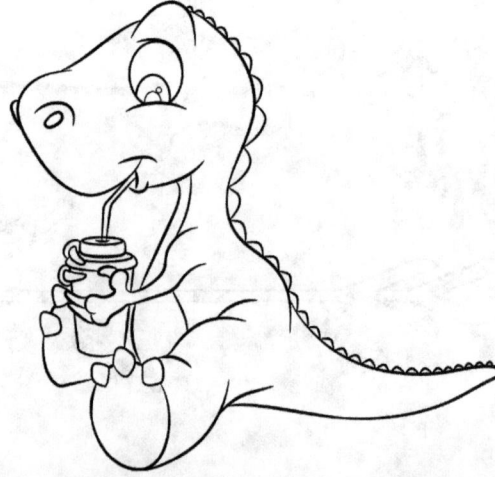

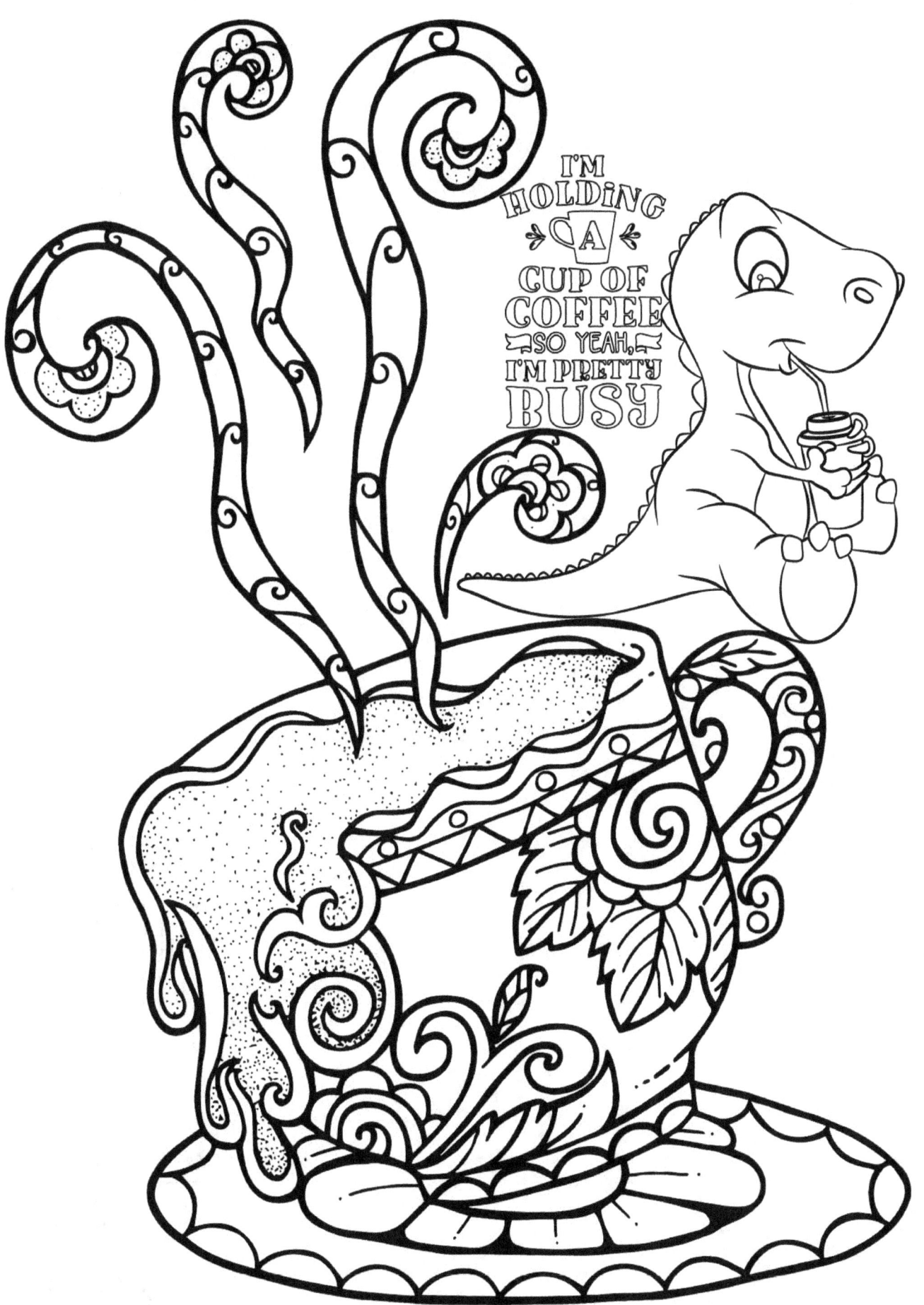

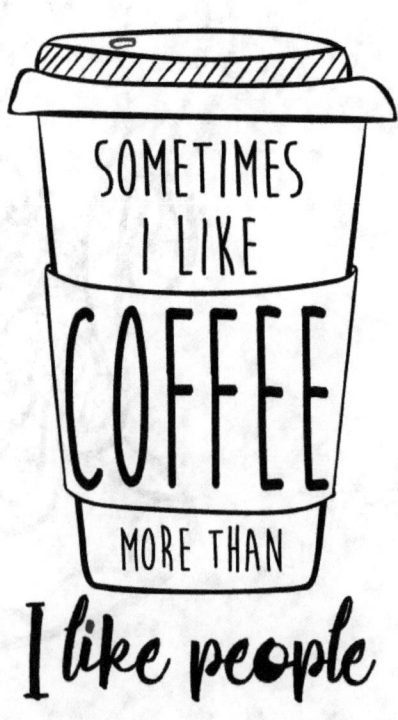

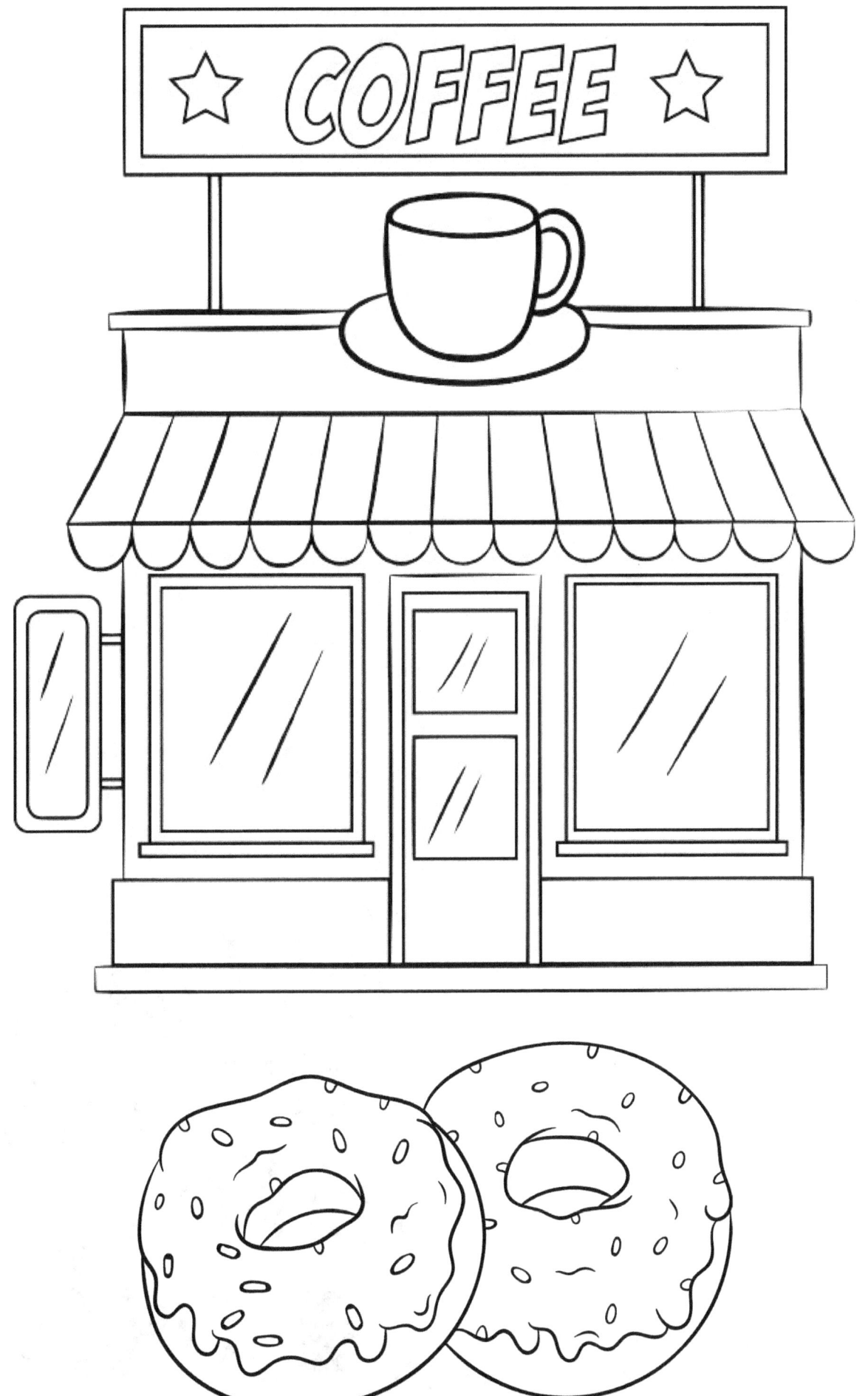

Everyone should believe in something. I believe I will have another coffee

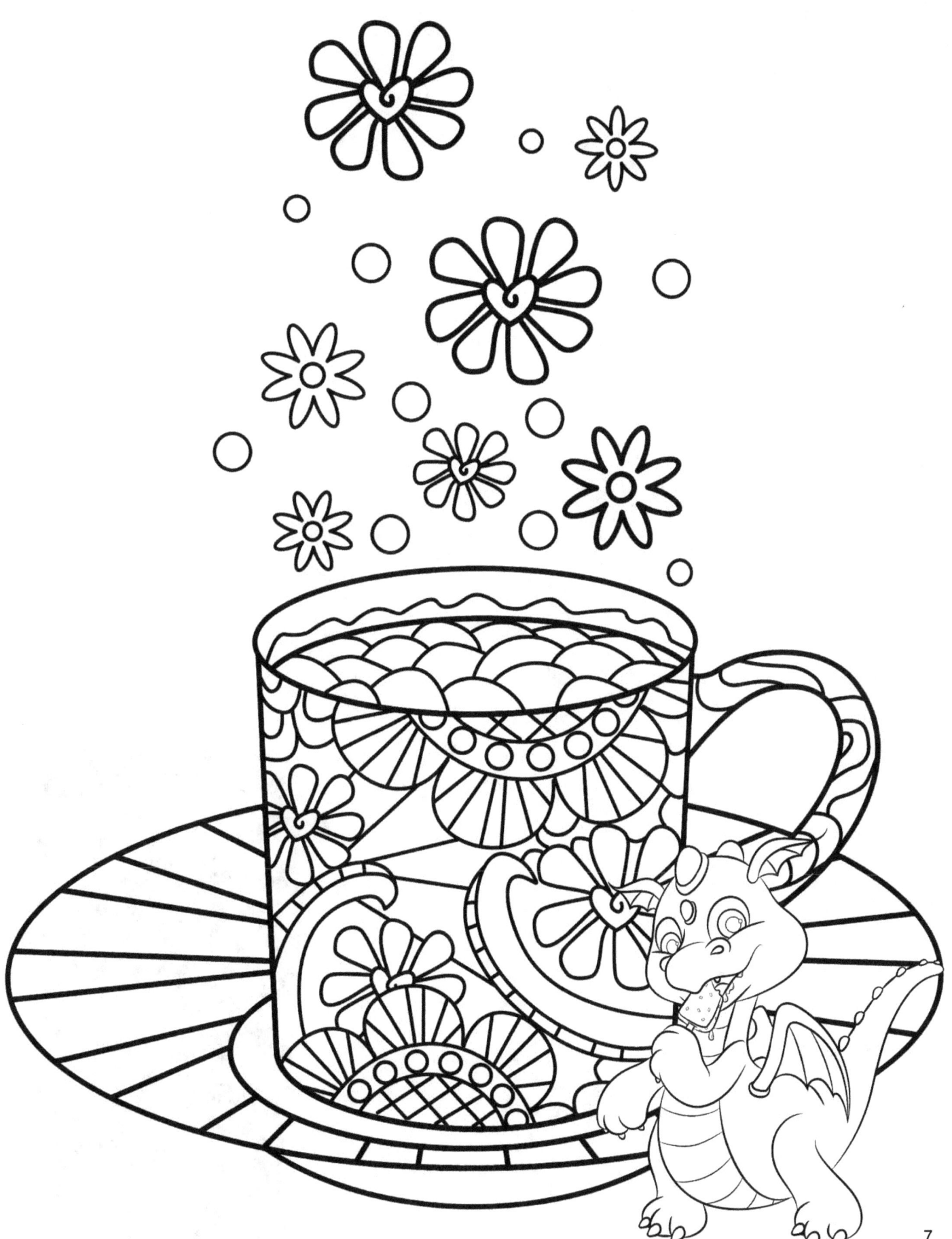

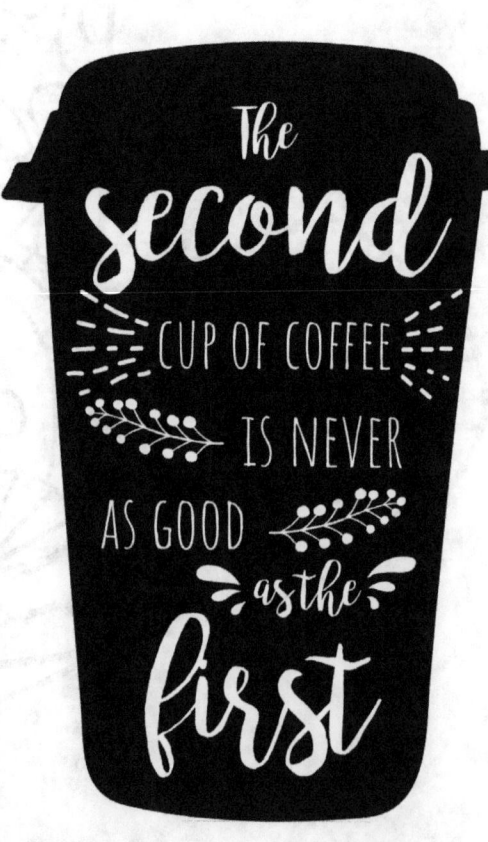

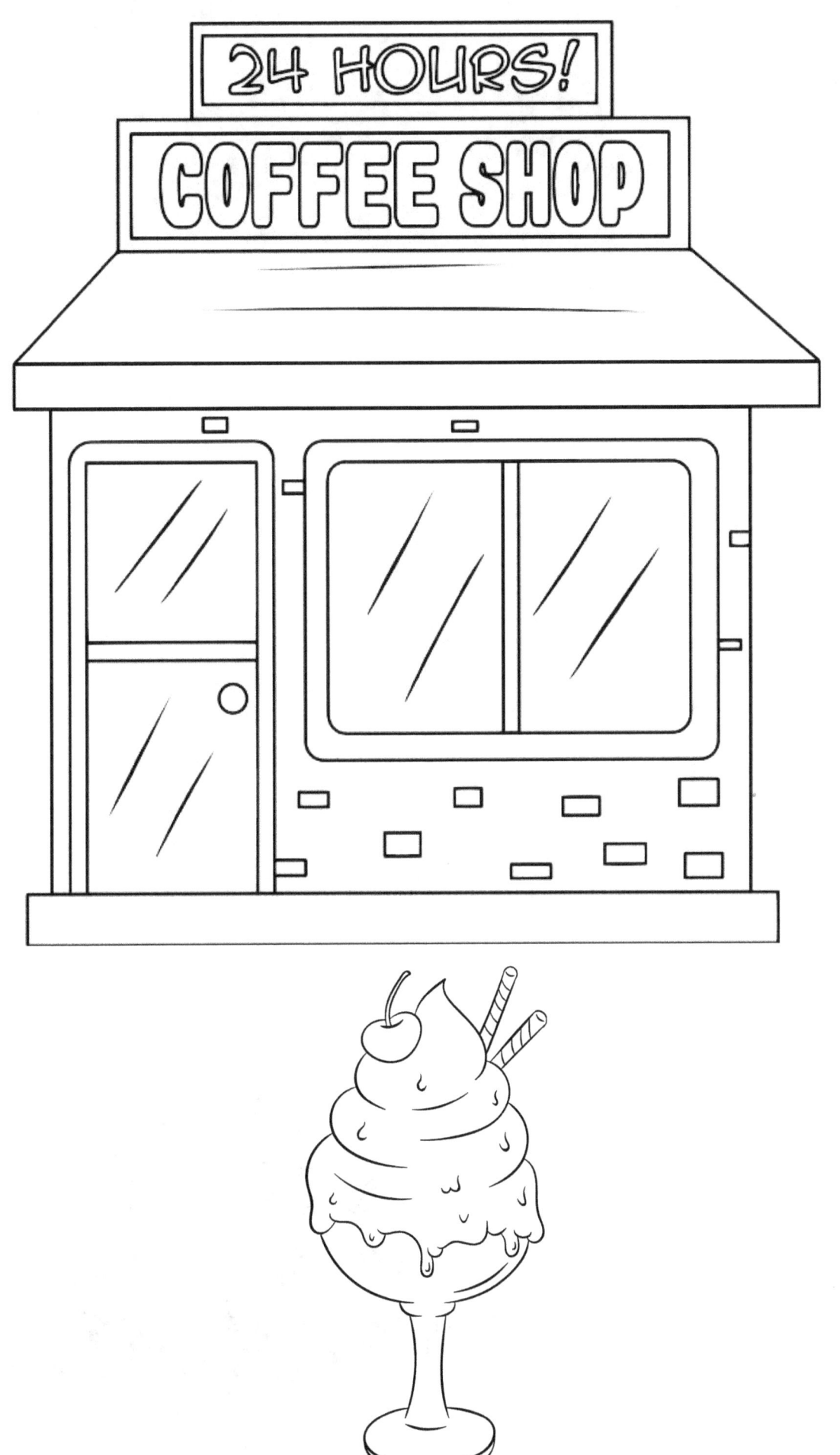

I'D RATHER TAKE coffee THAN compliments JUST NOW

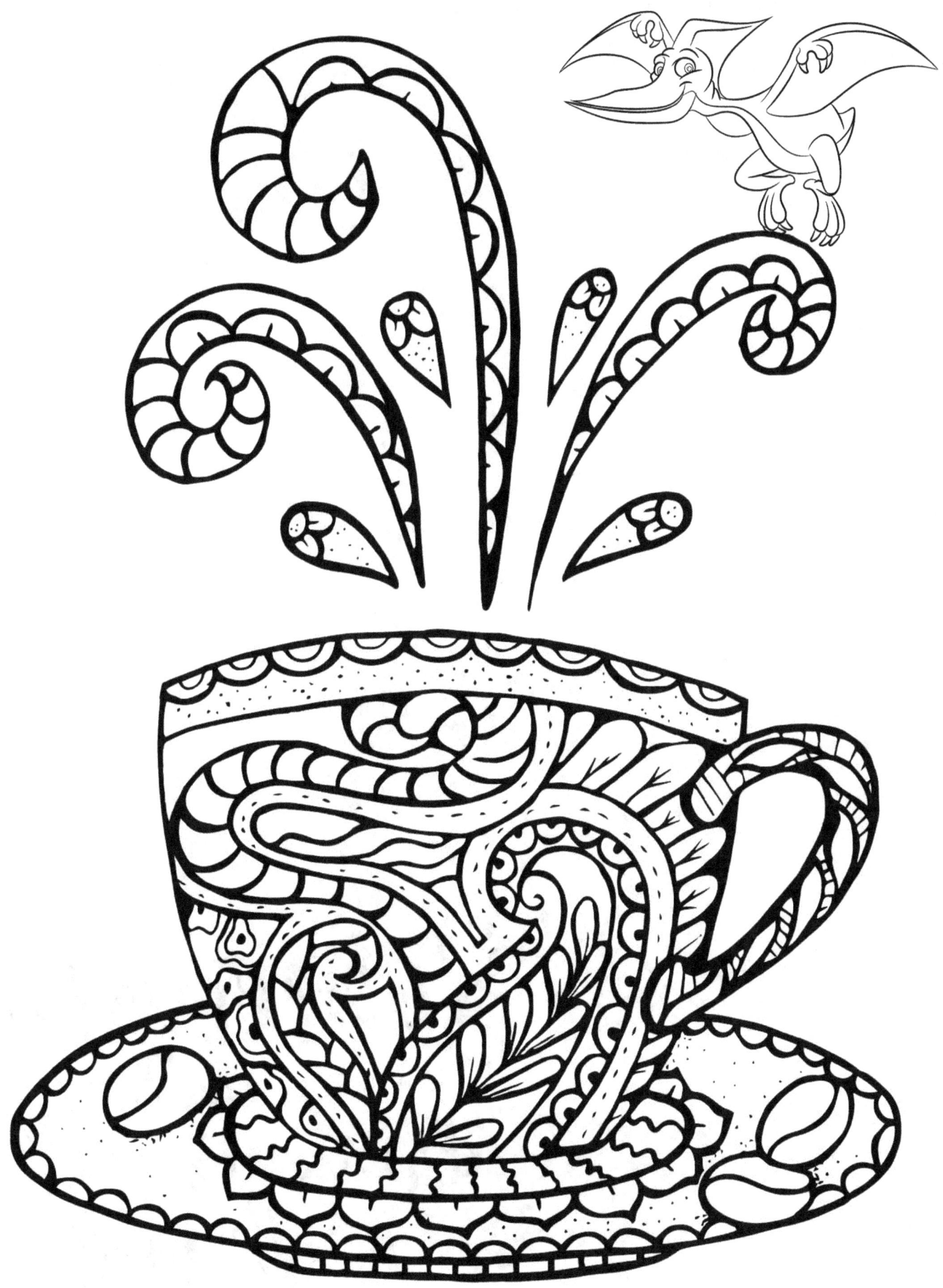

Sometimes
I GO HOURS *without*
drinking coffee
IT'S CALLED sleeping

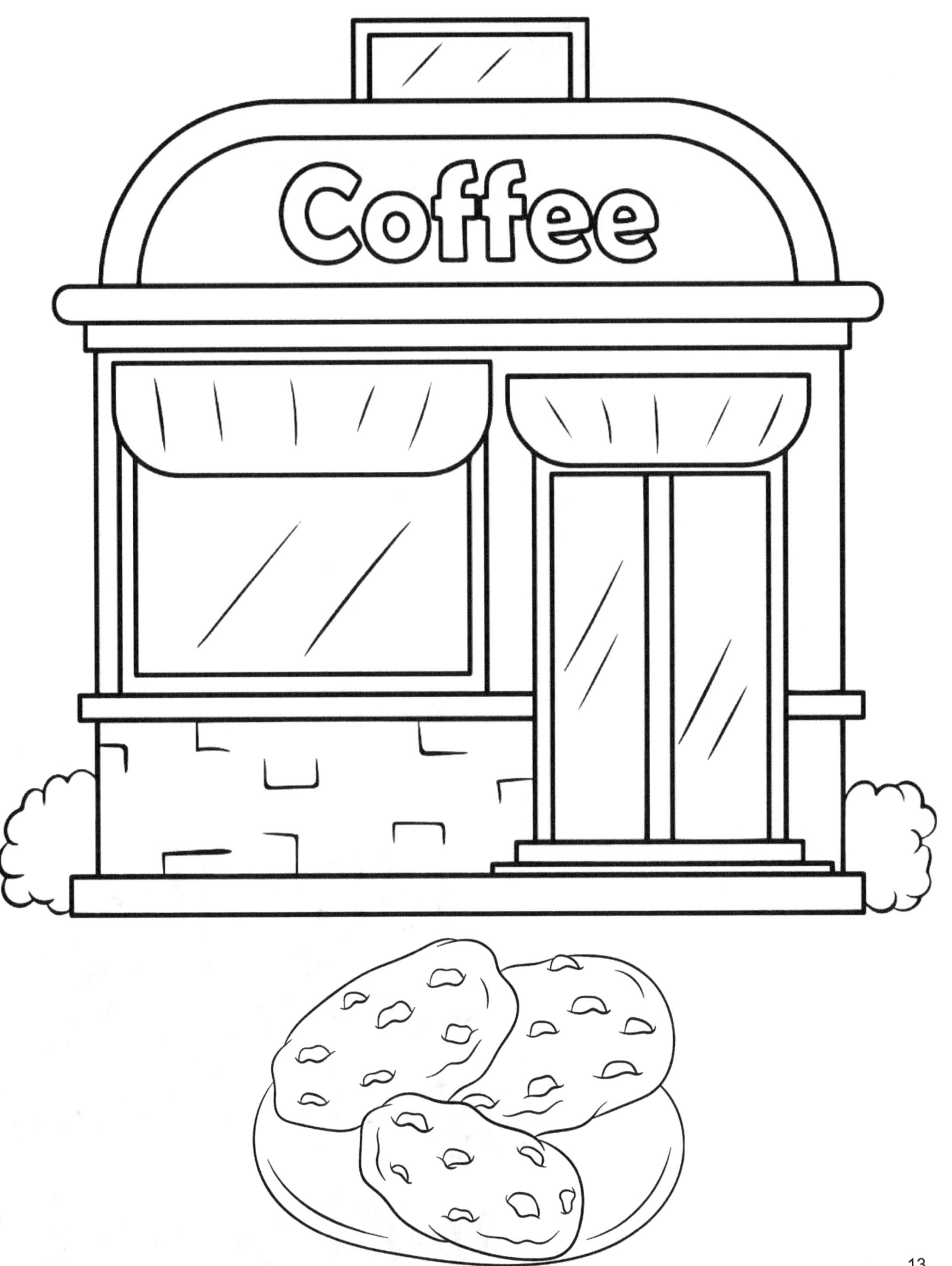

I like coffee because gives me the illusion that might be awake

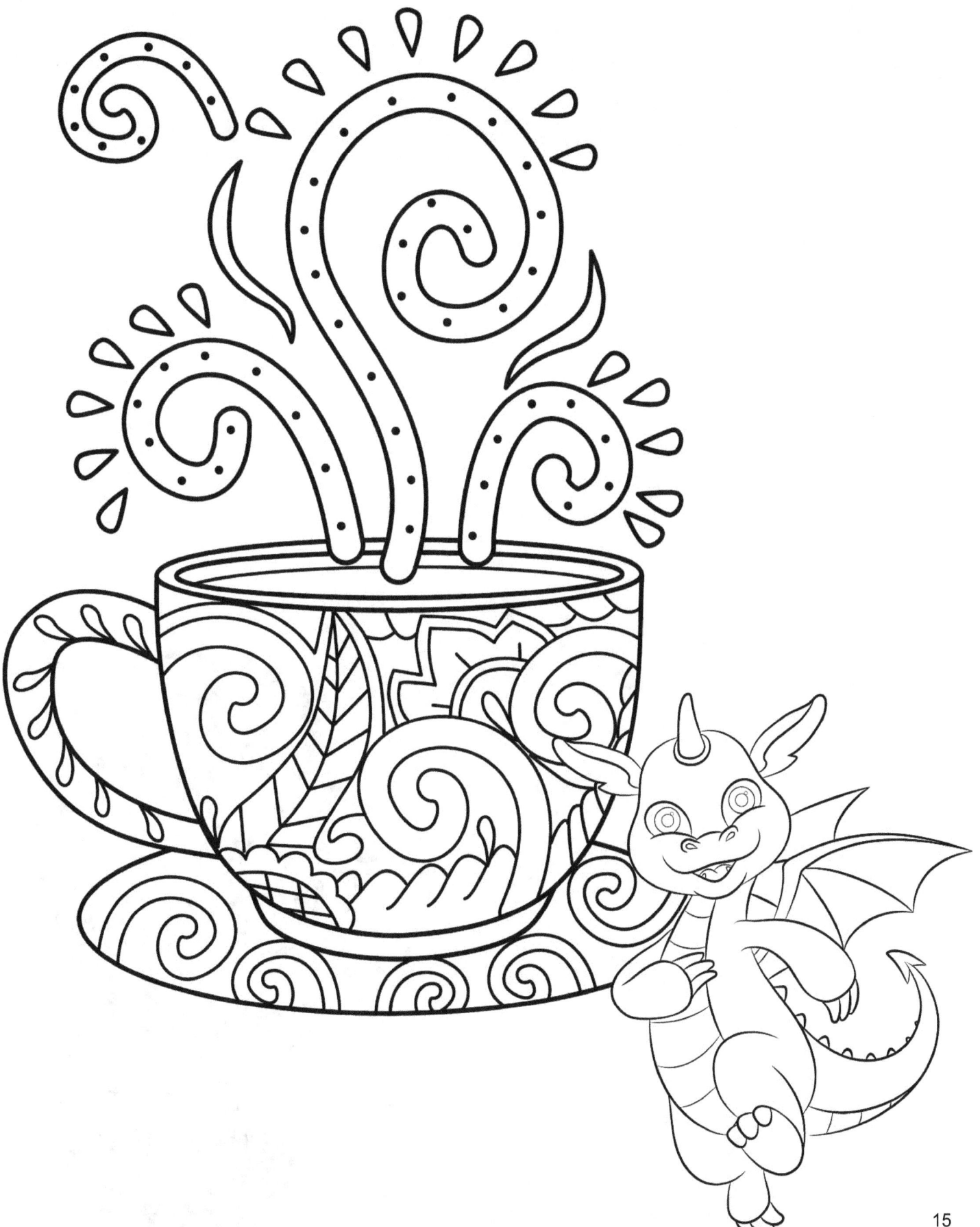

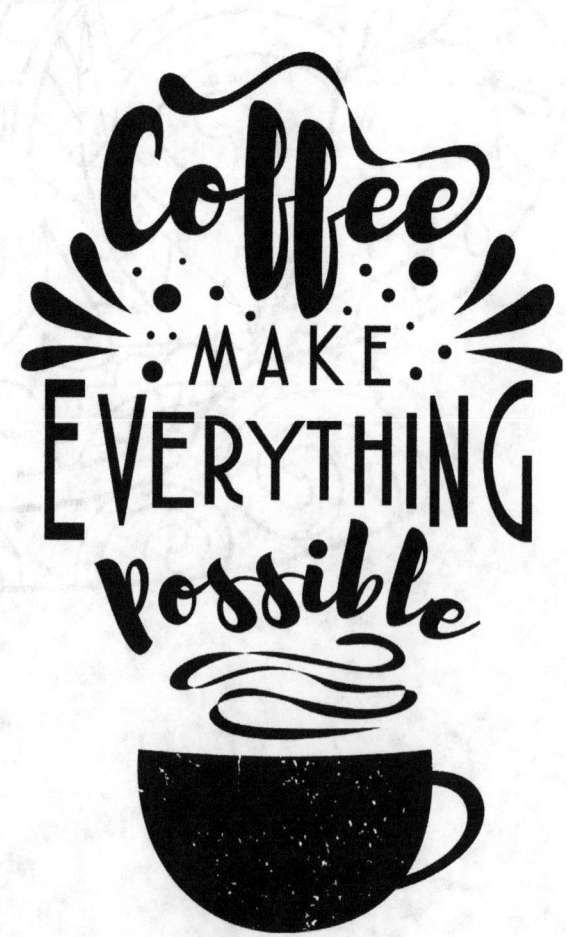

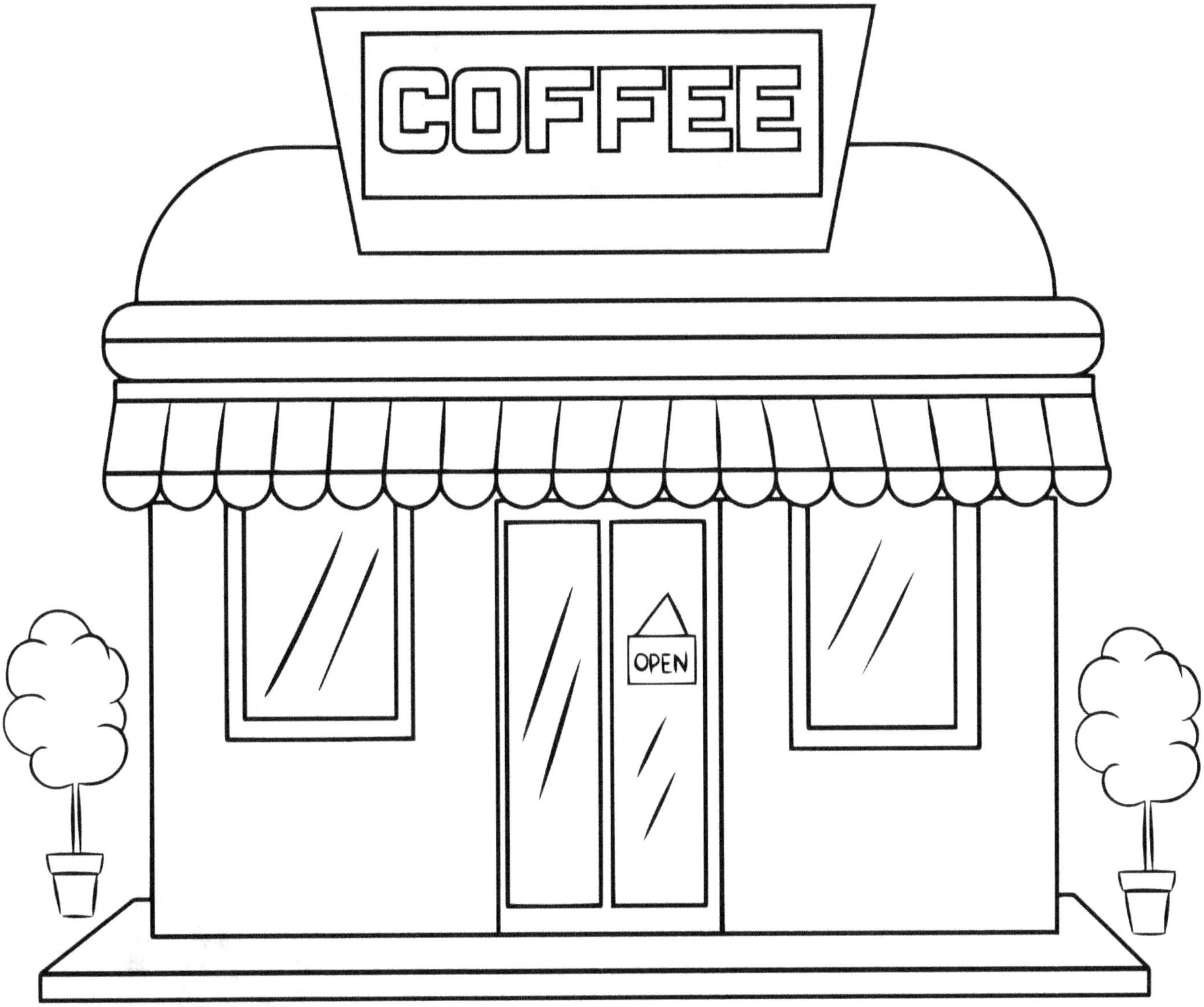

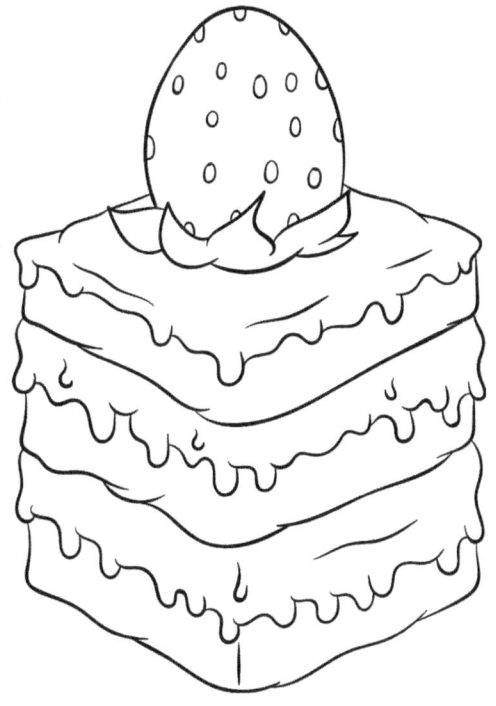

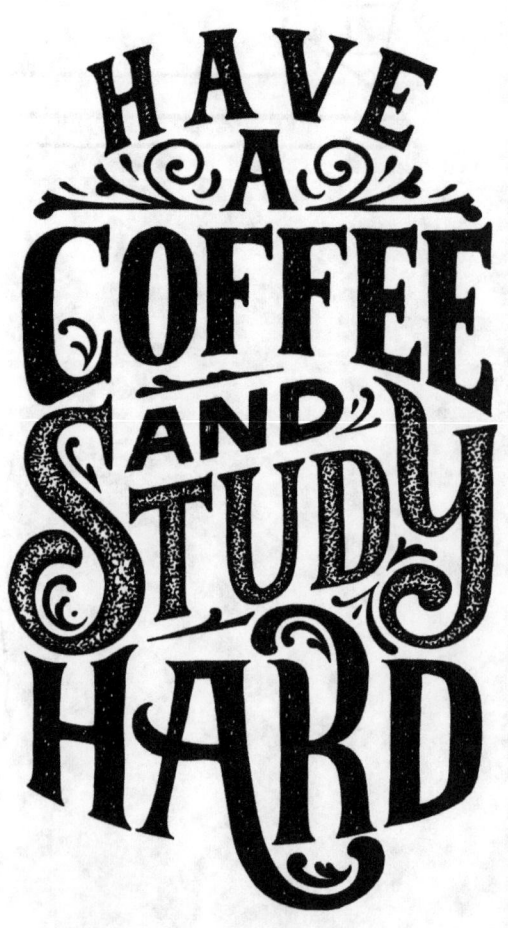

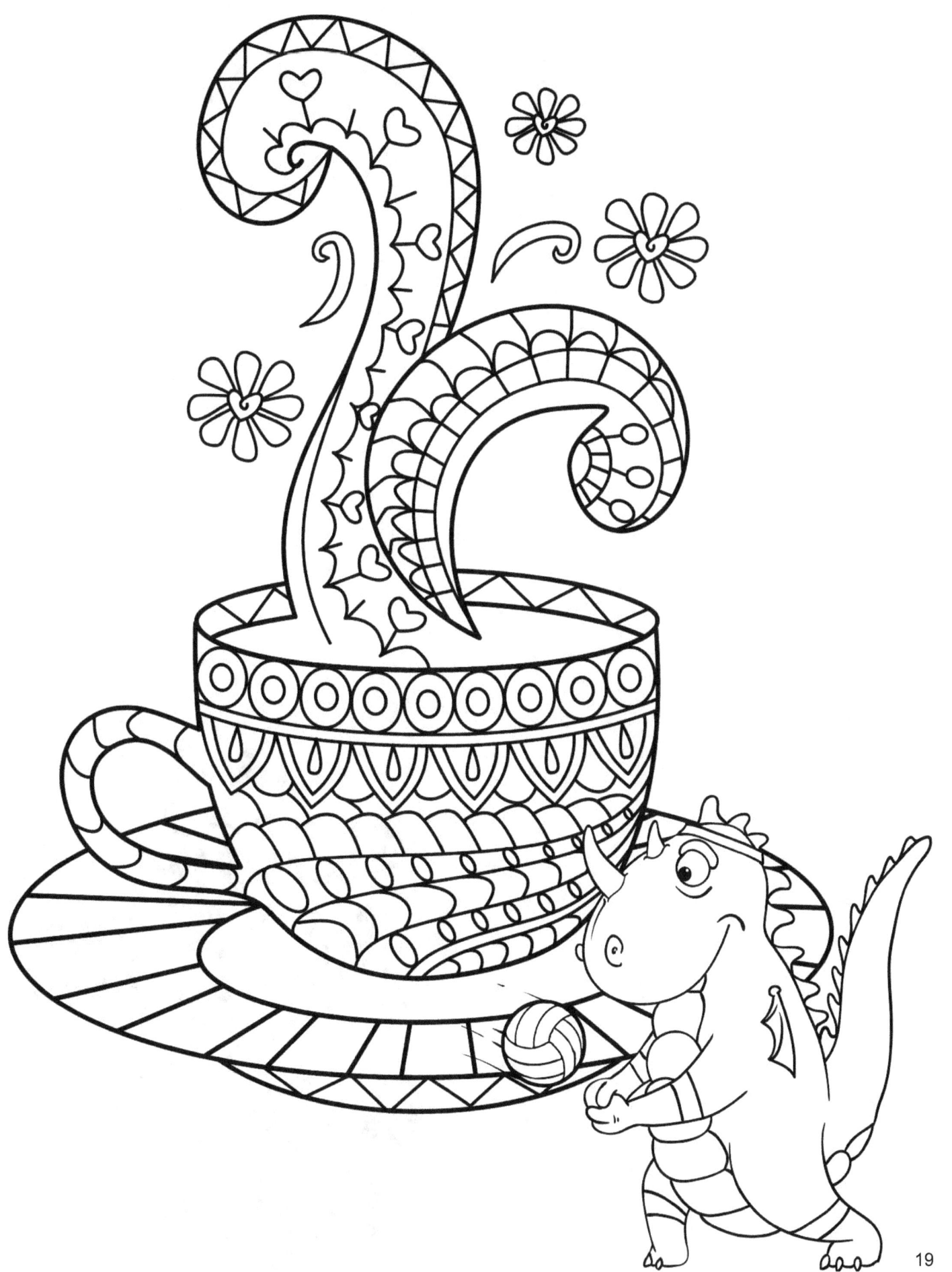

Always Start Your Day With a Coffee

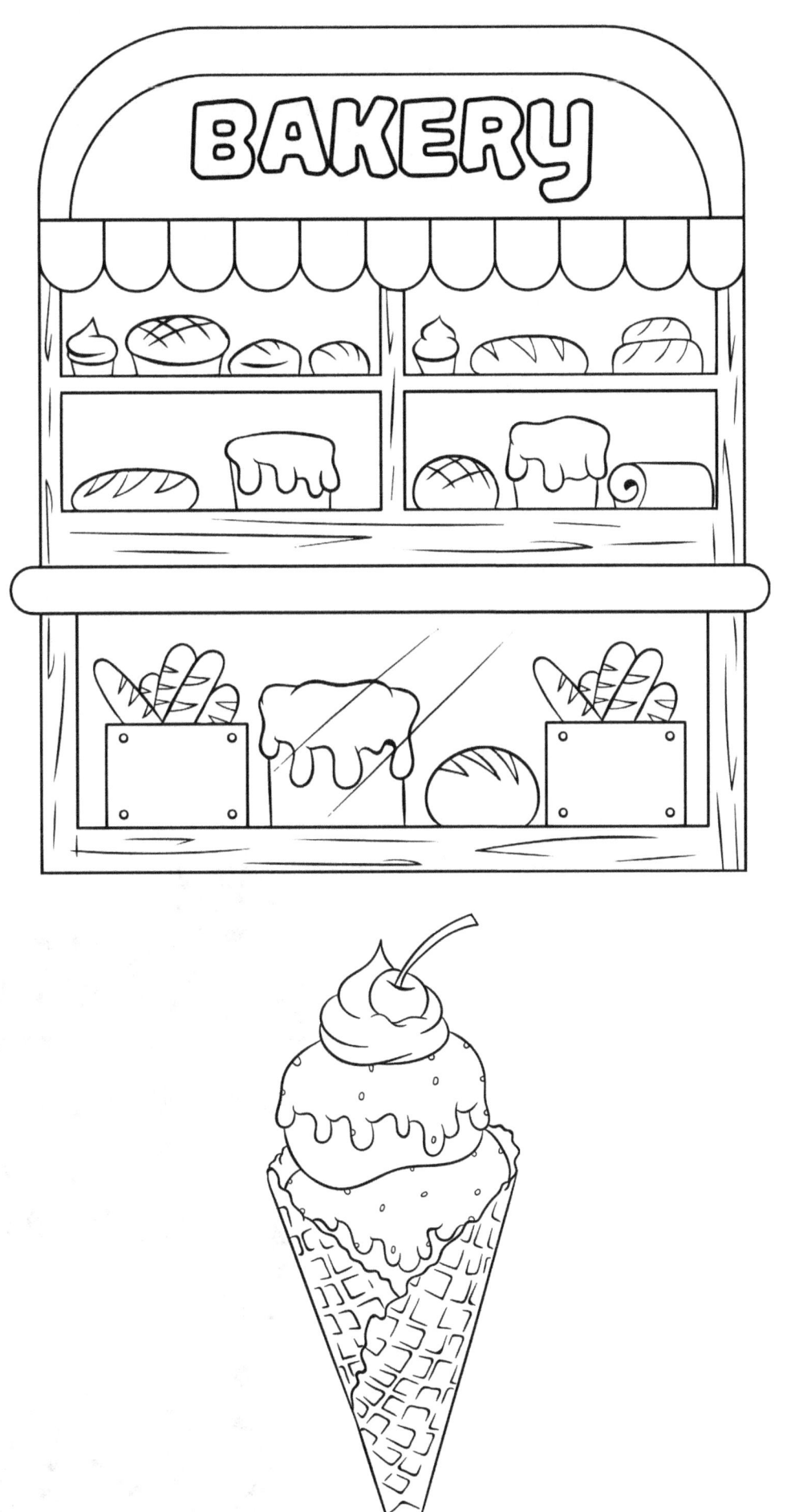

Change the World Start with Coffee

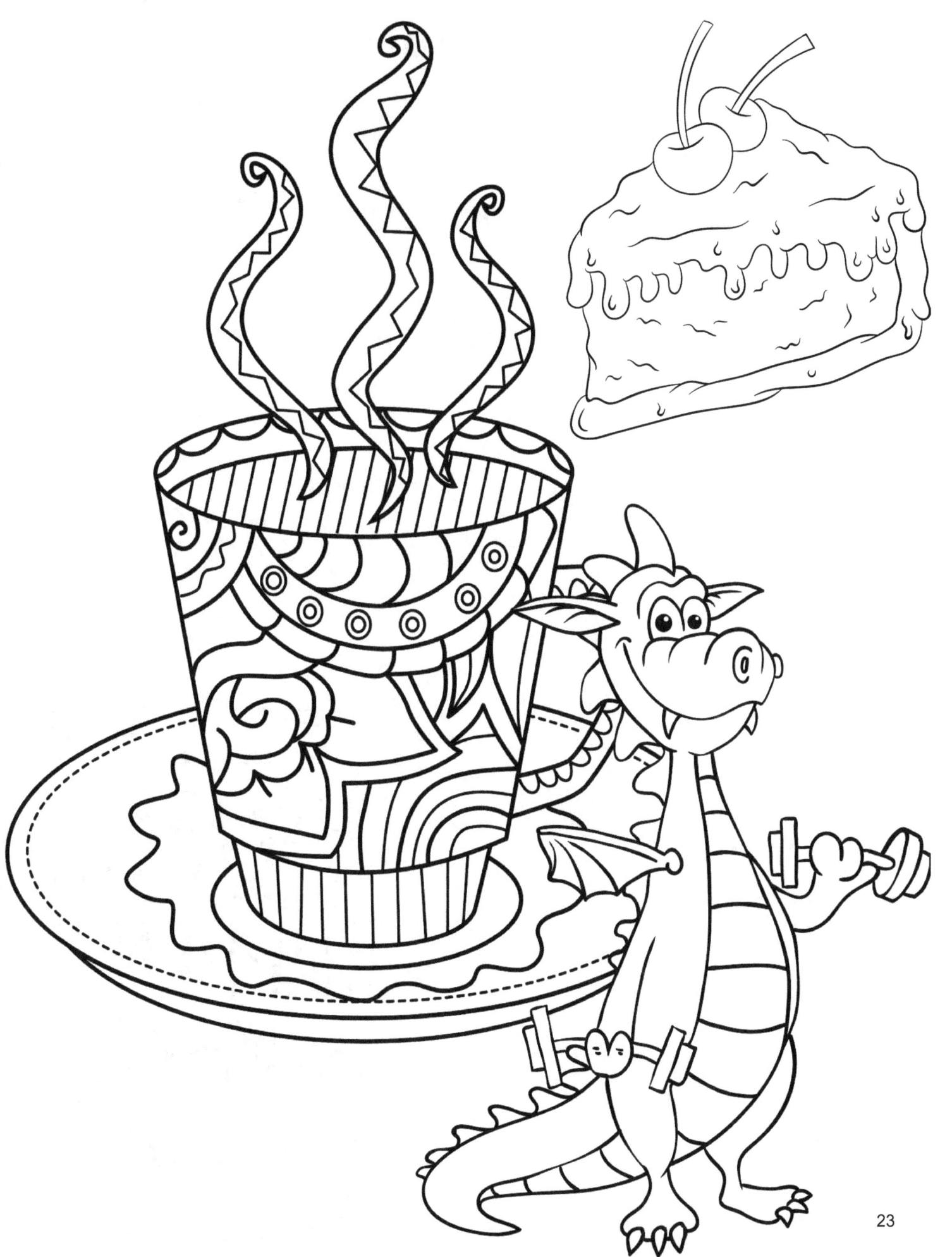

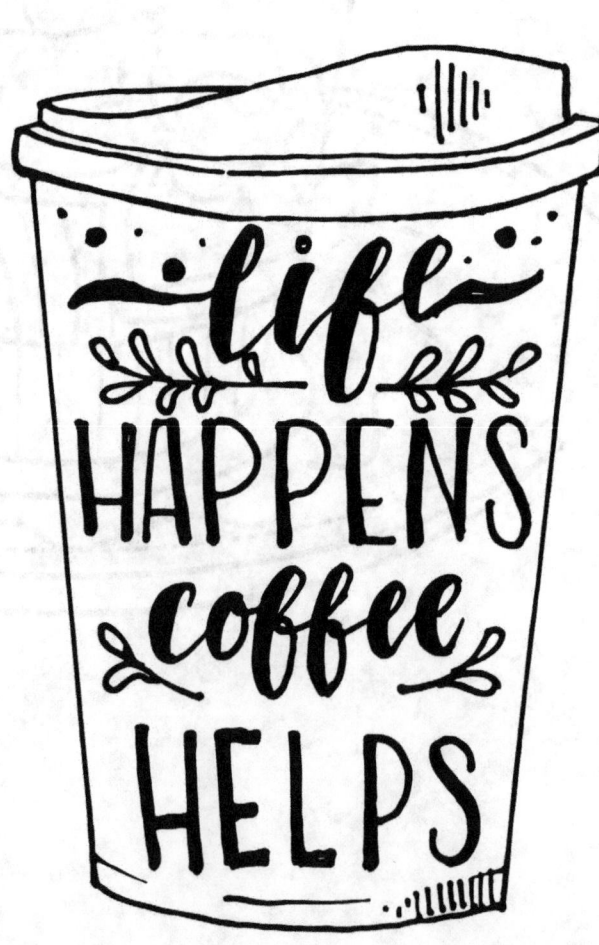

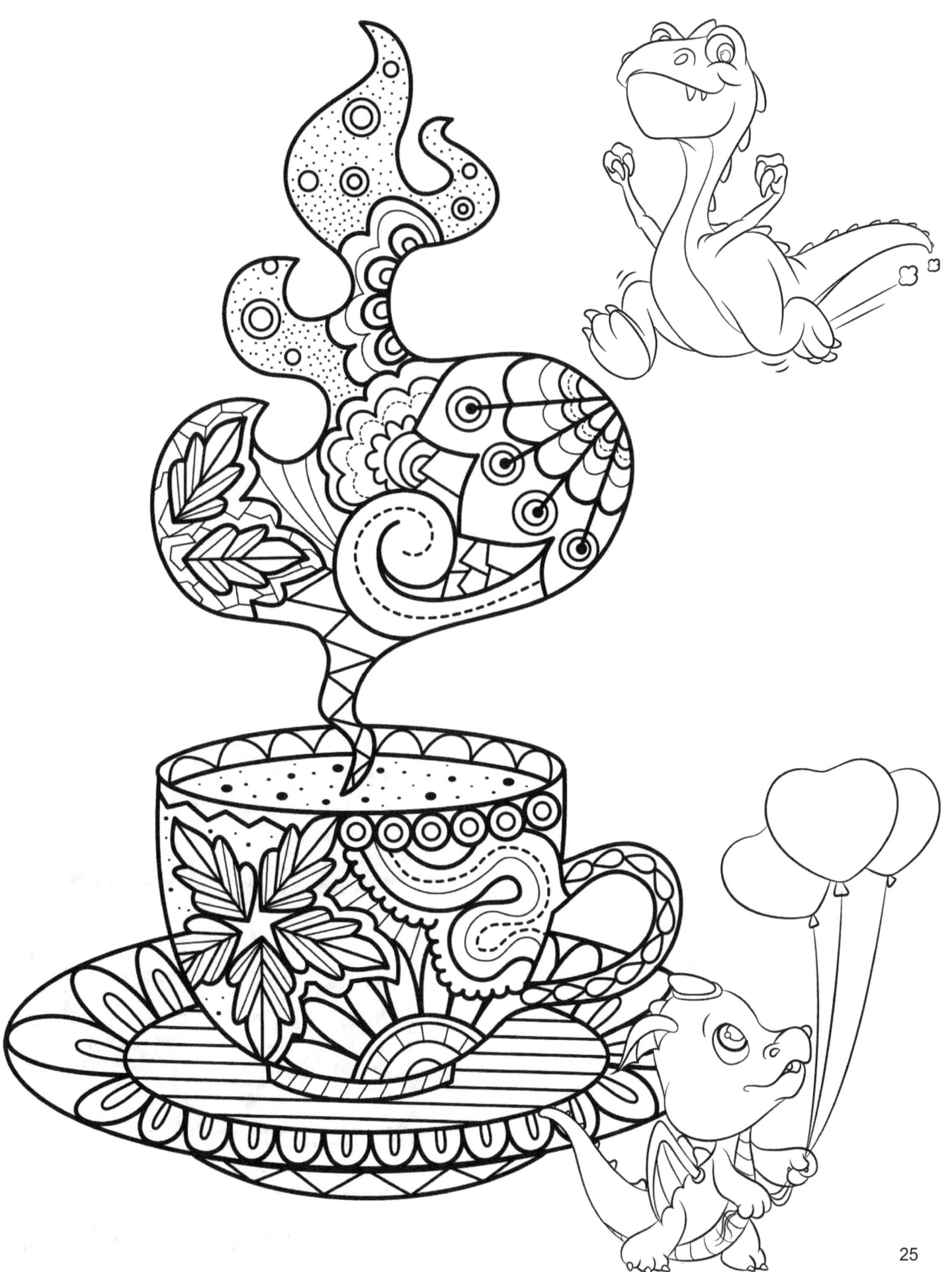

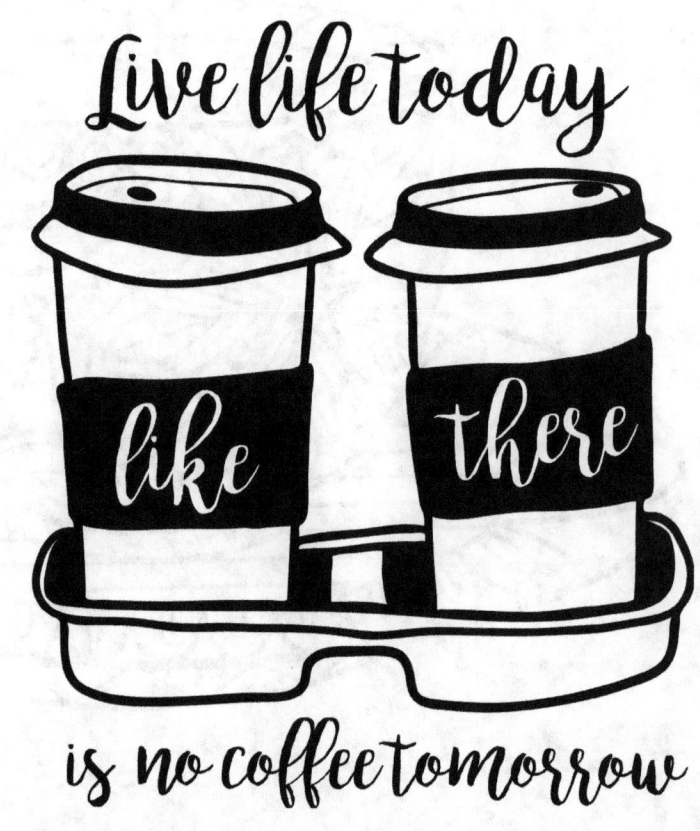

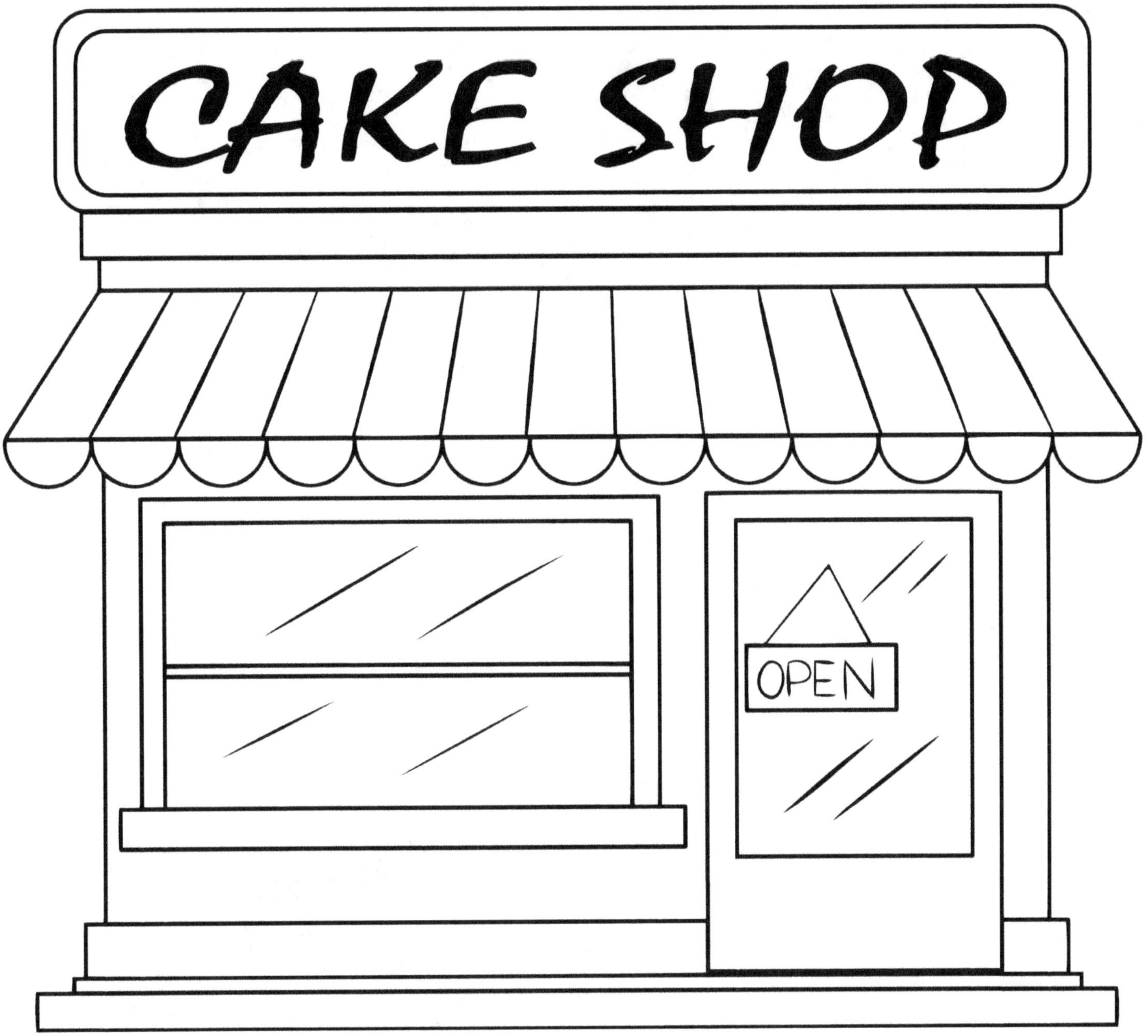

CAKE SHOP

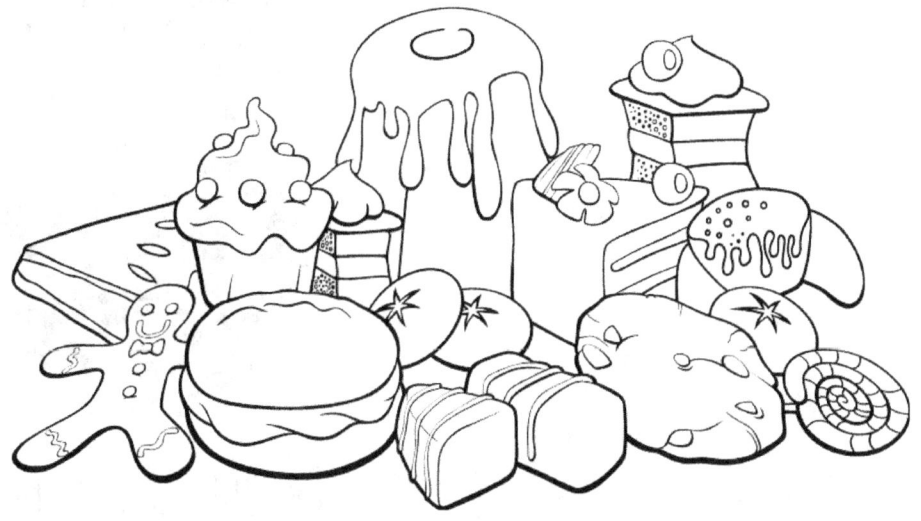

AS LONG AS
THERE WAS COFFEE
in the world,

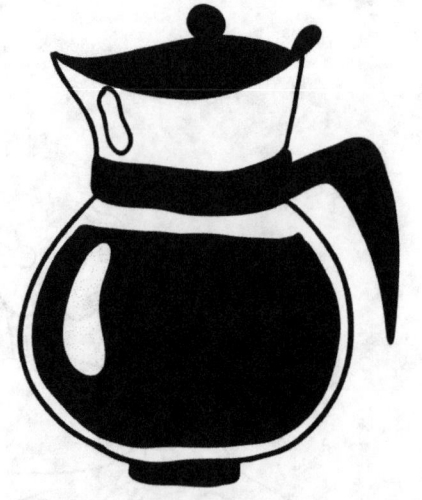

HOW BAD COULD THINGS BE?

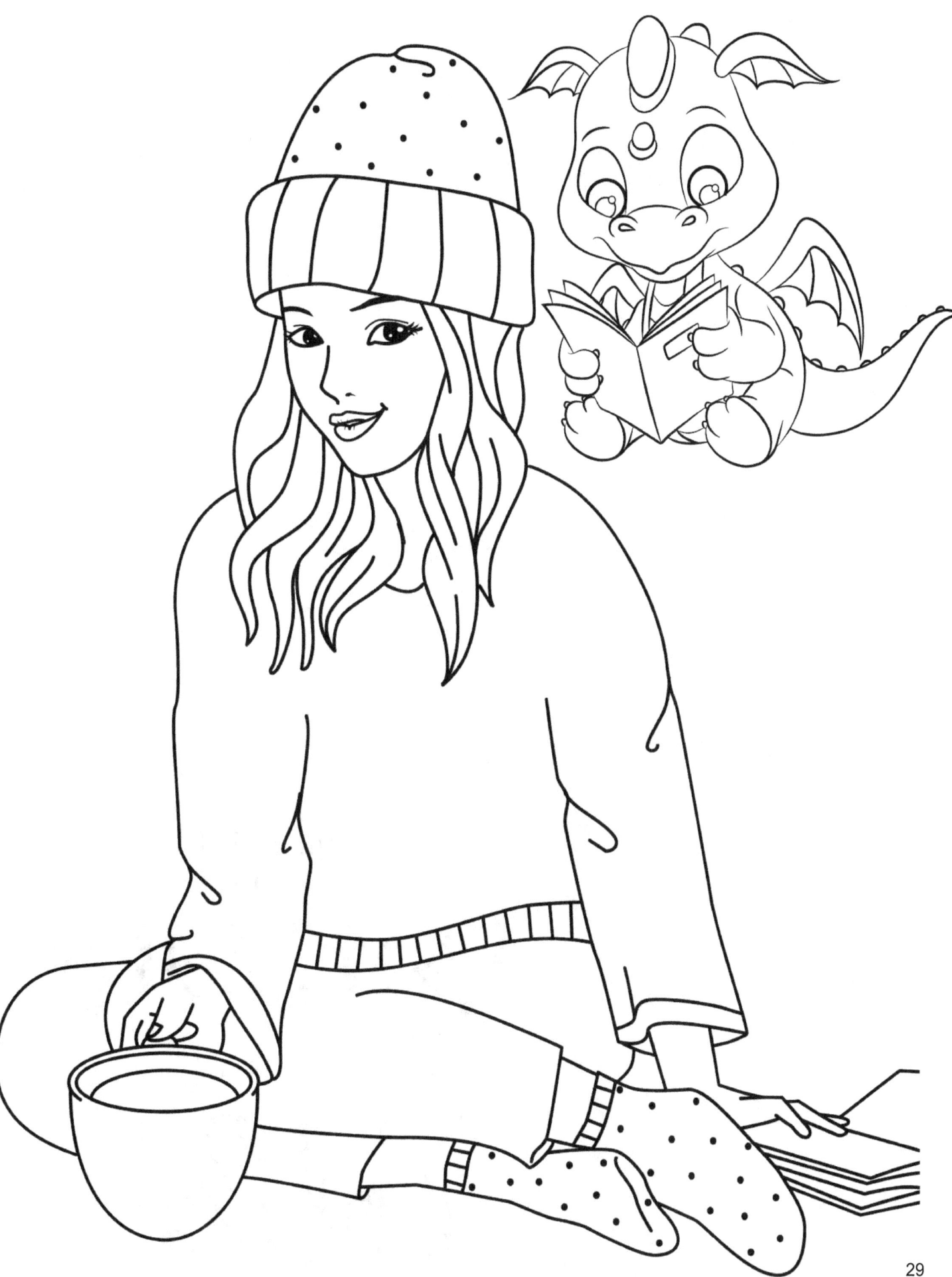

I WANT
someone
TO LOOK AT ME
THE WAY I LOOK AT
coffee

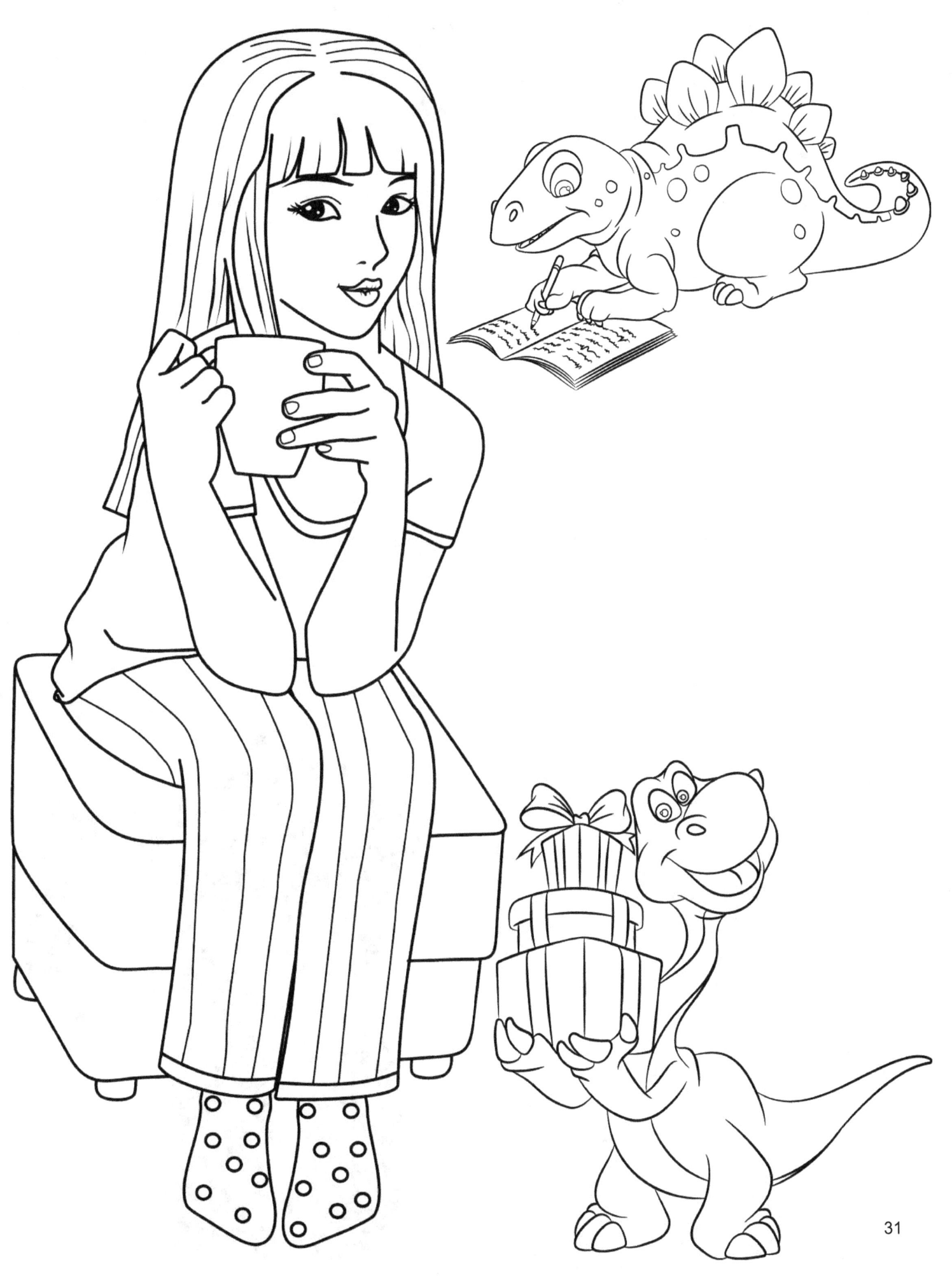

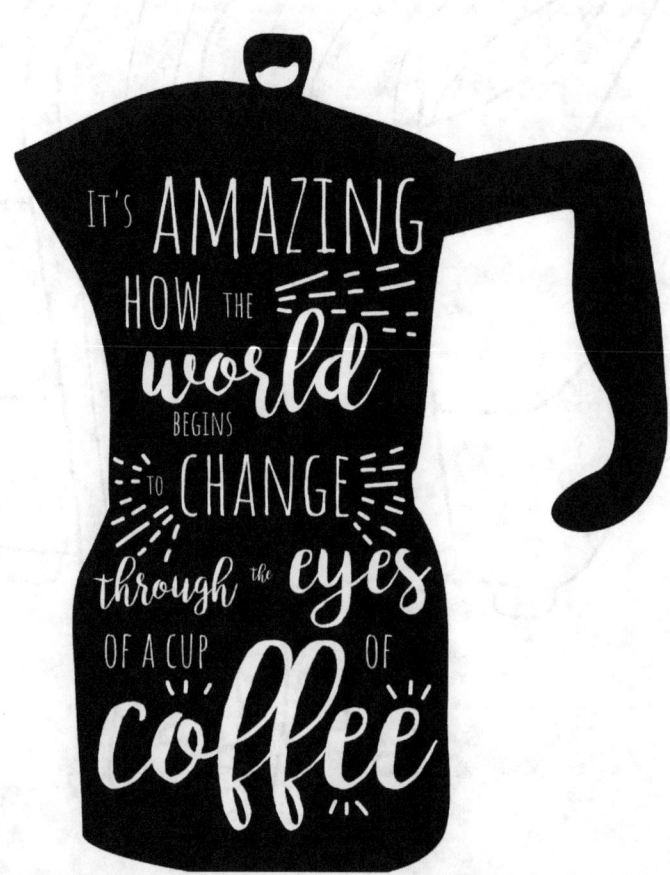

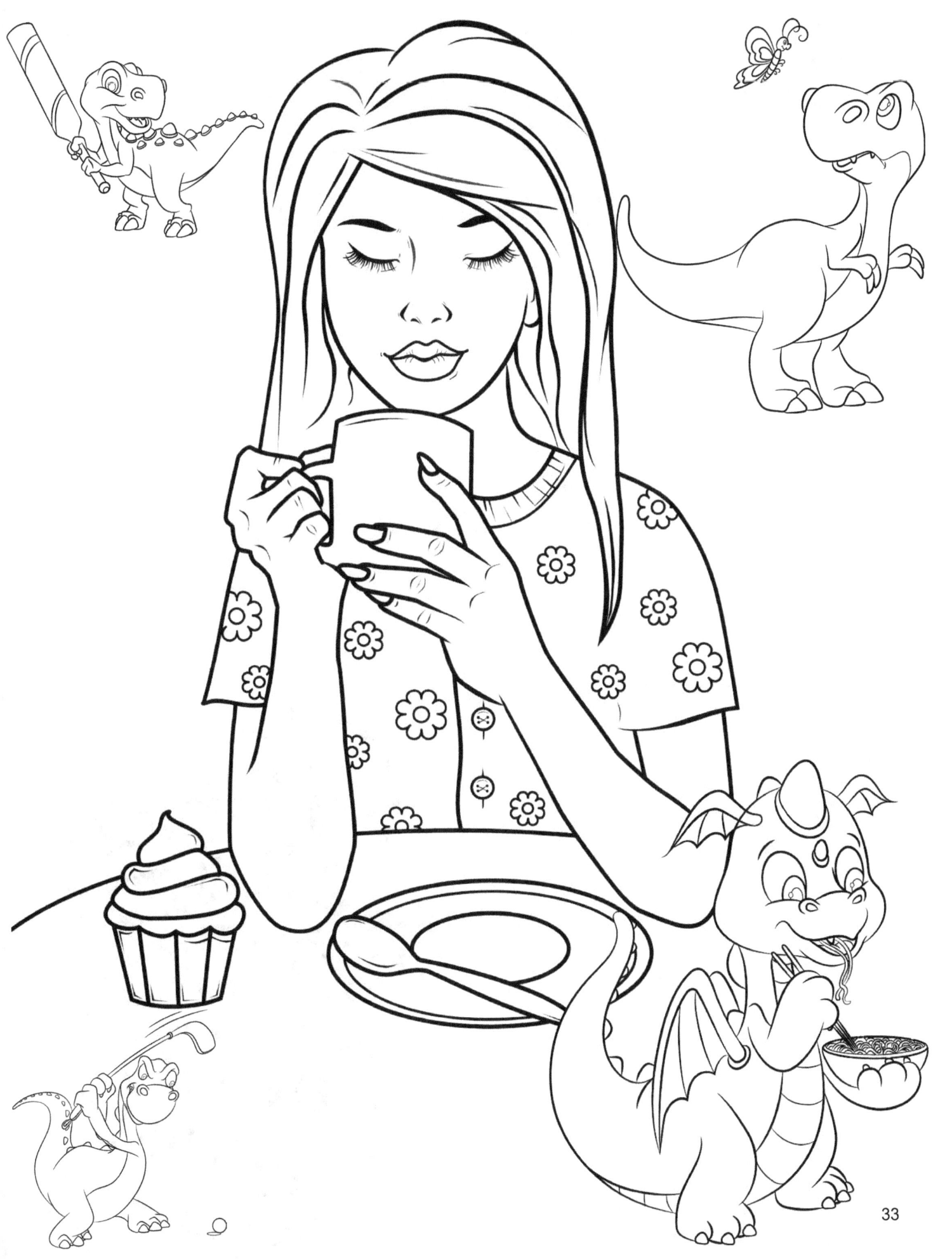

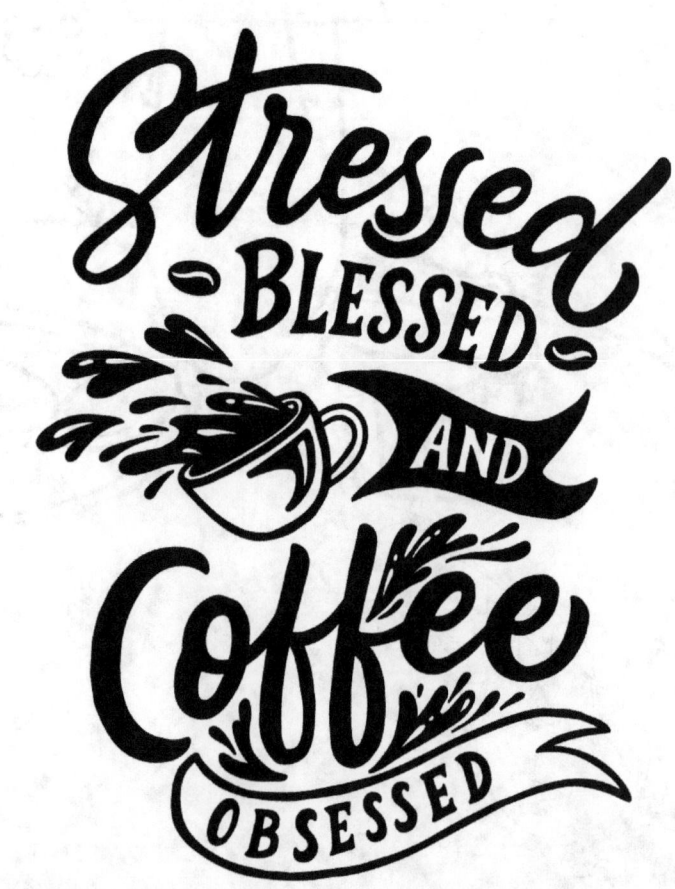

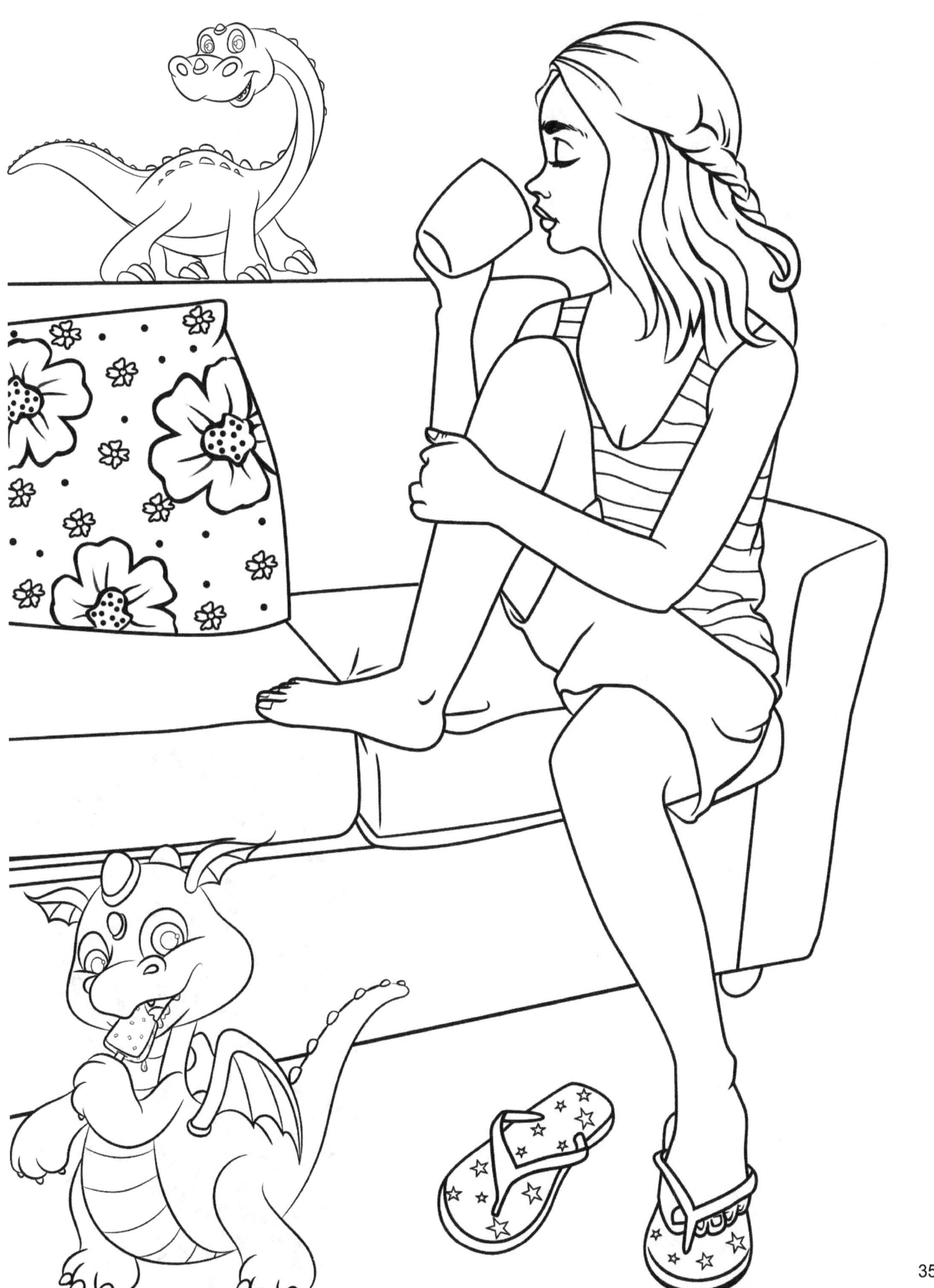

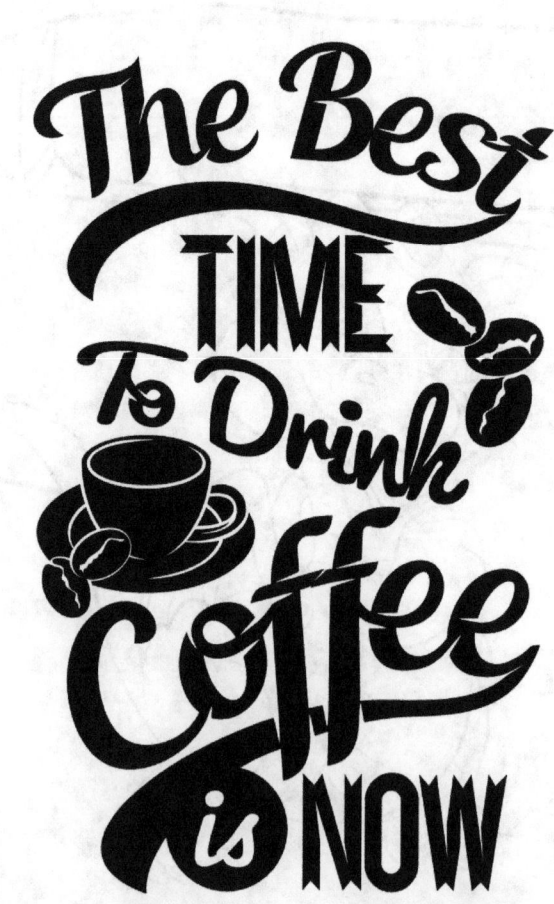

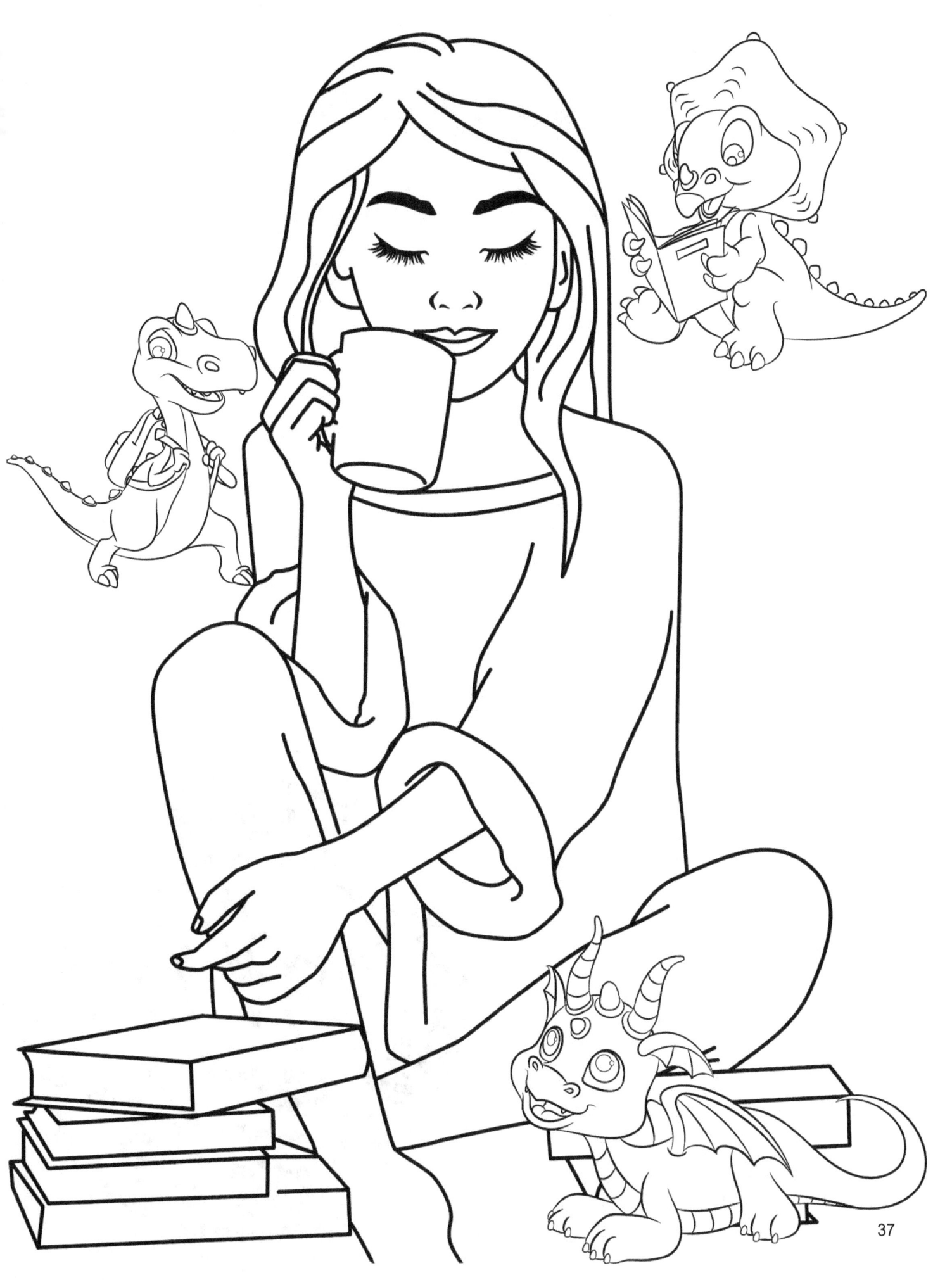

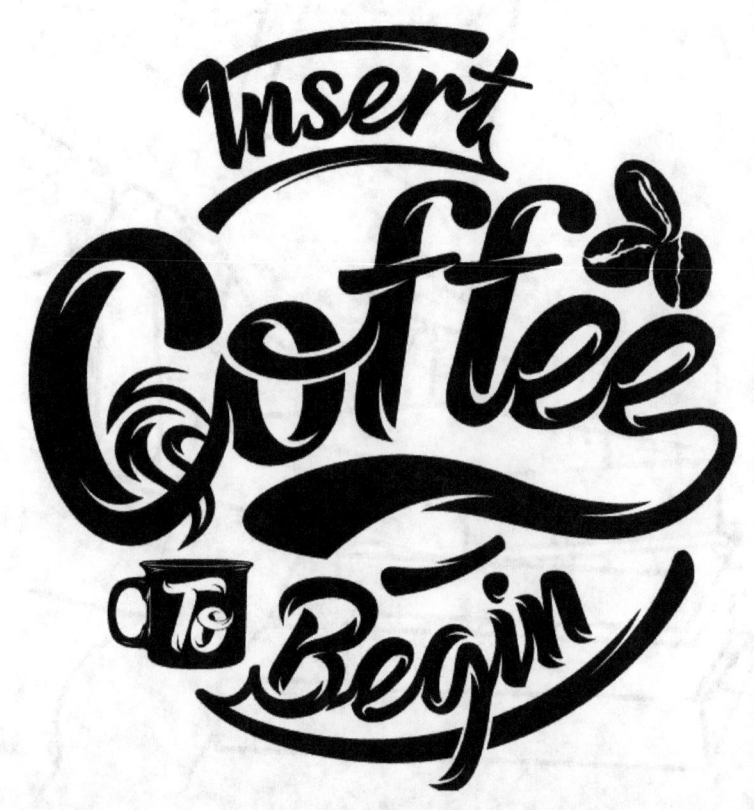

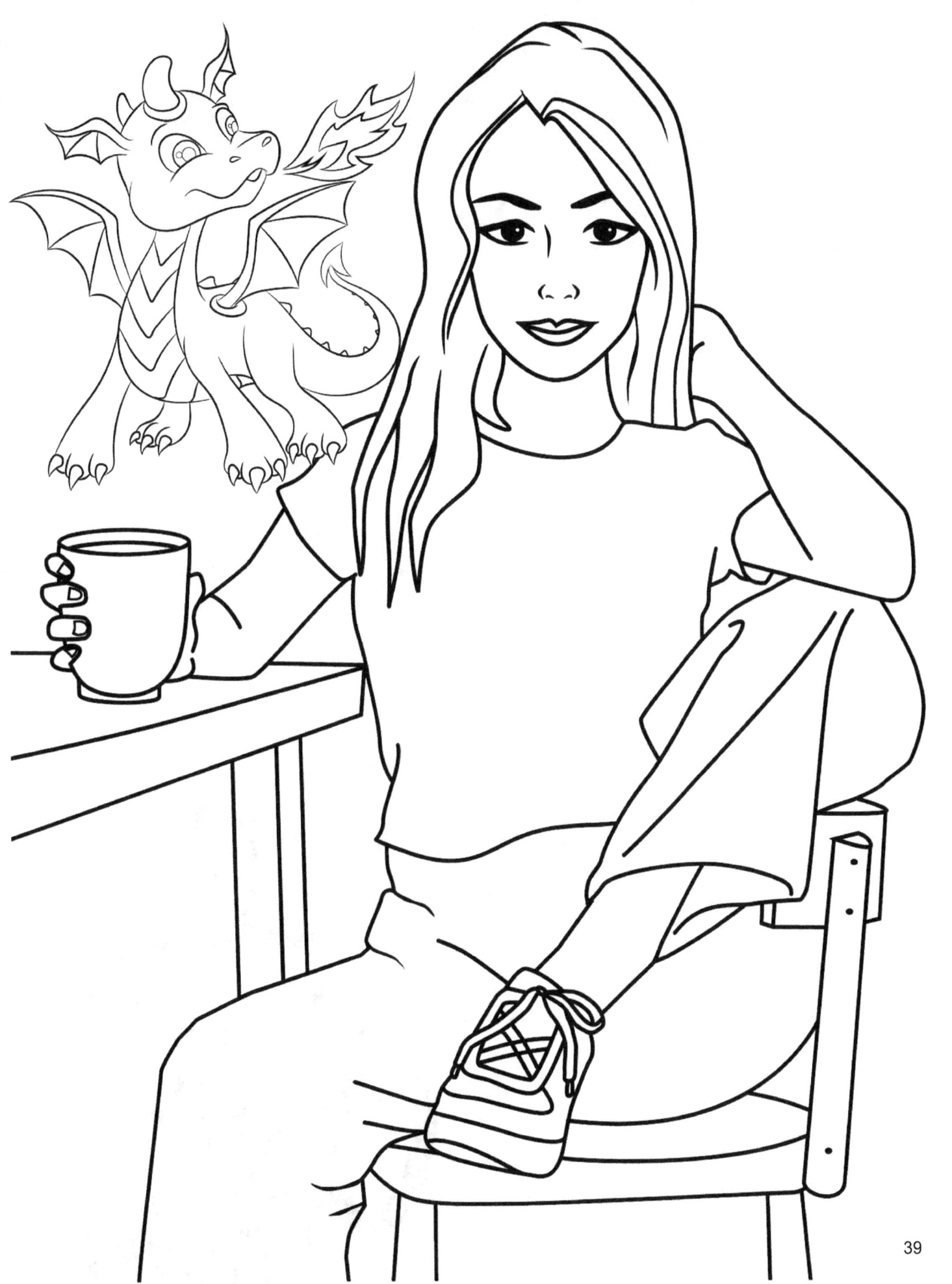

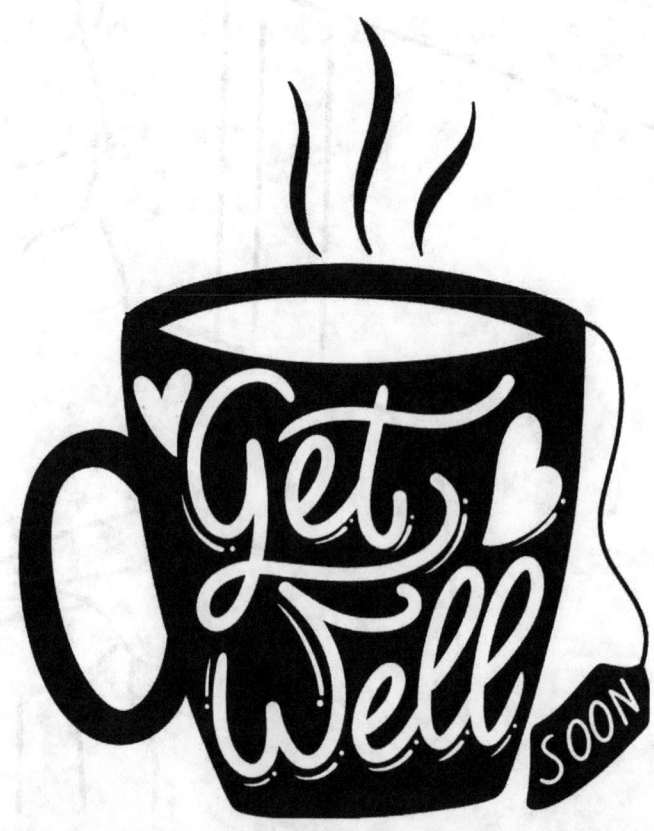

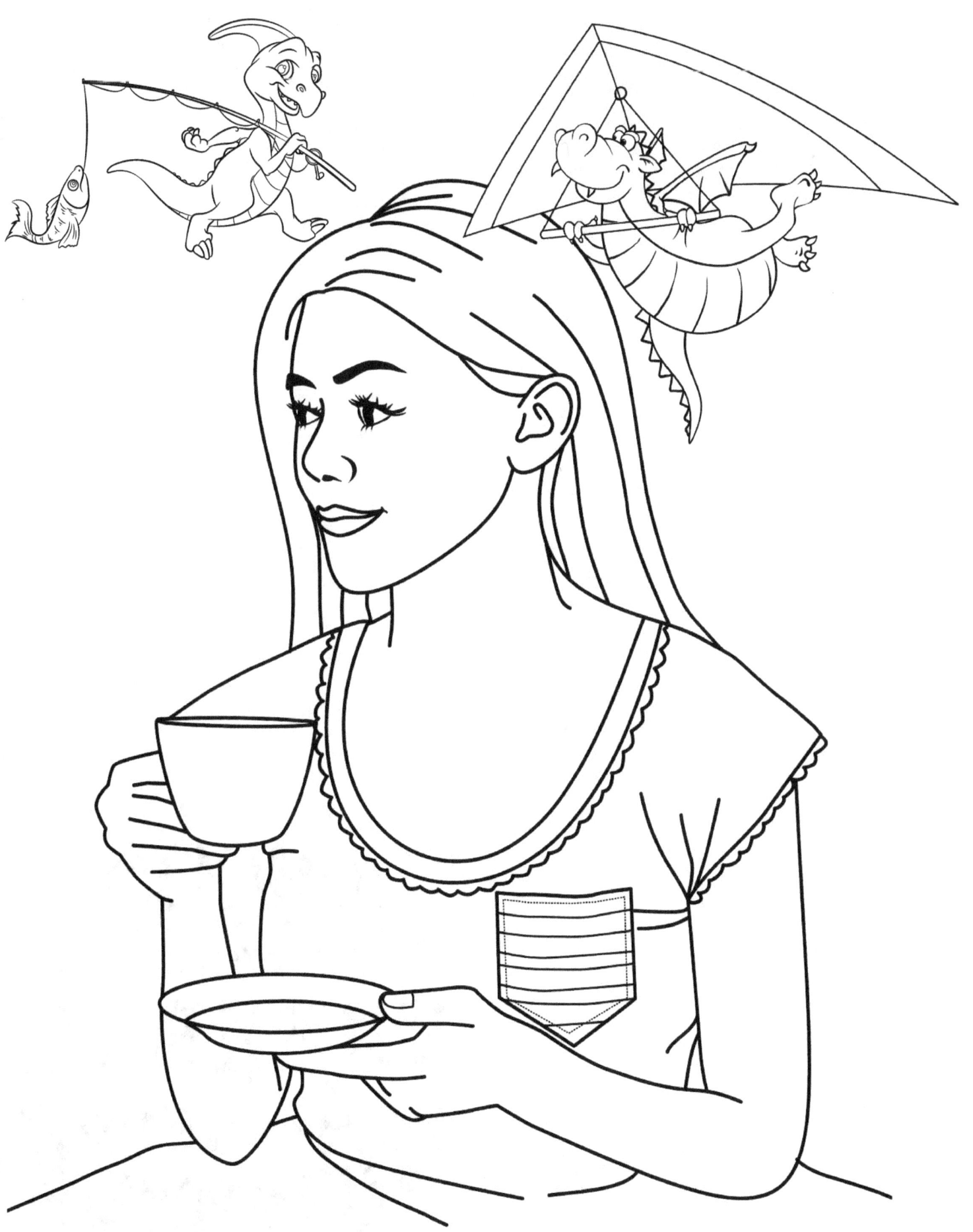

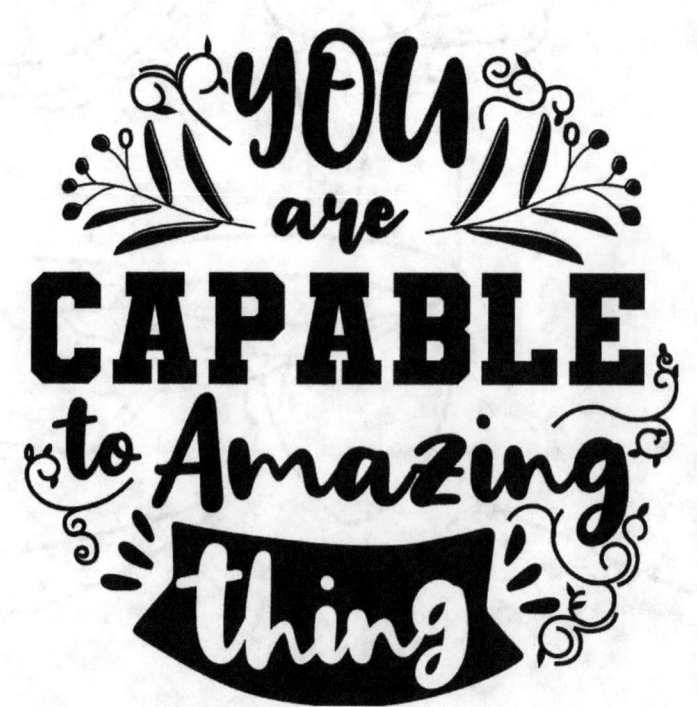

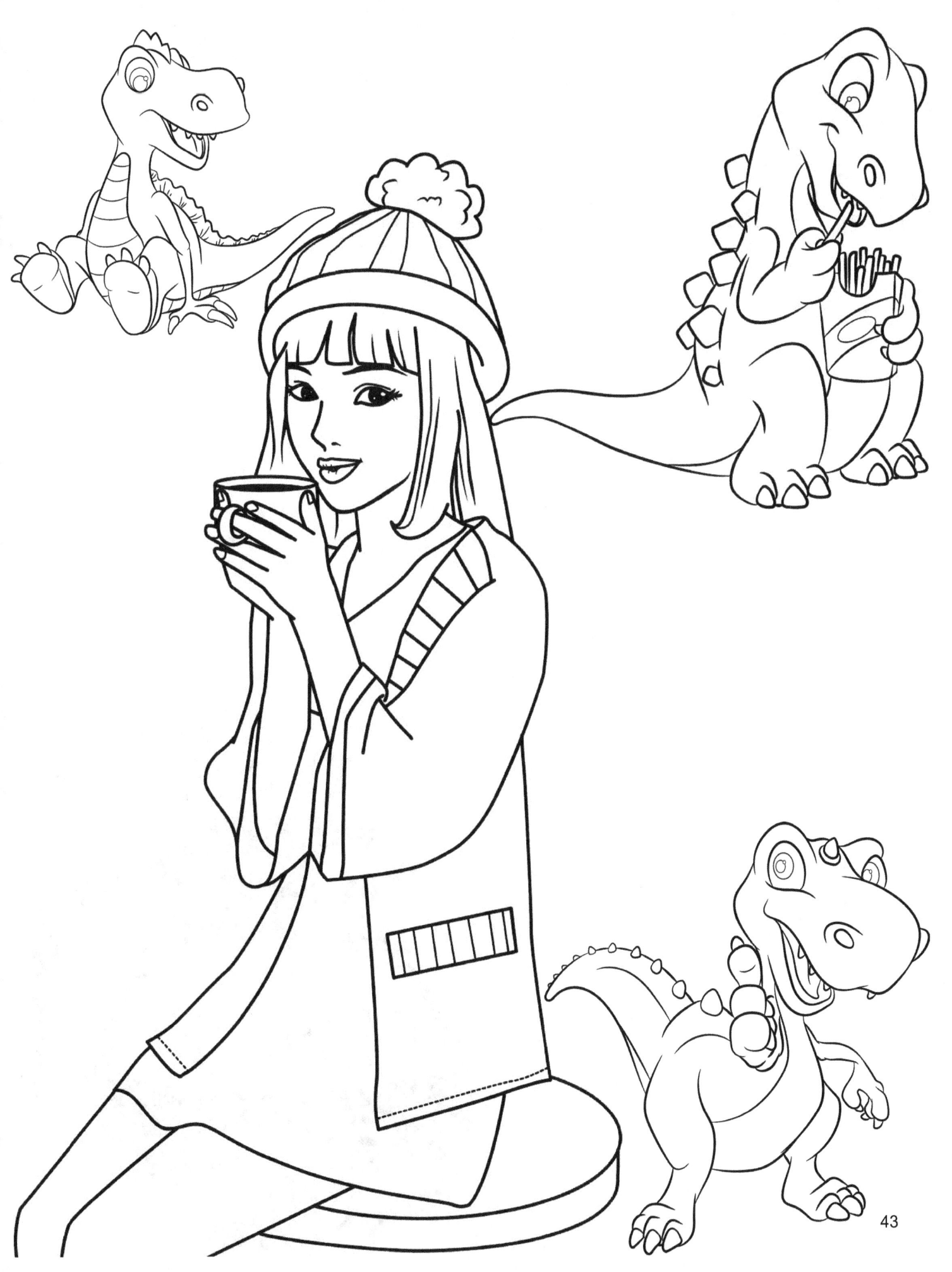

LOVE IS IN THE AIR, and IT SMELLS LIKE COFFEE

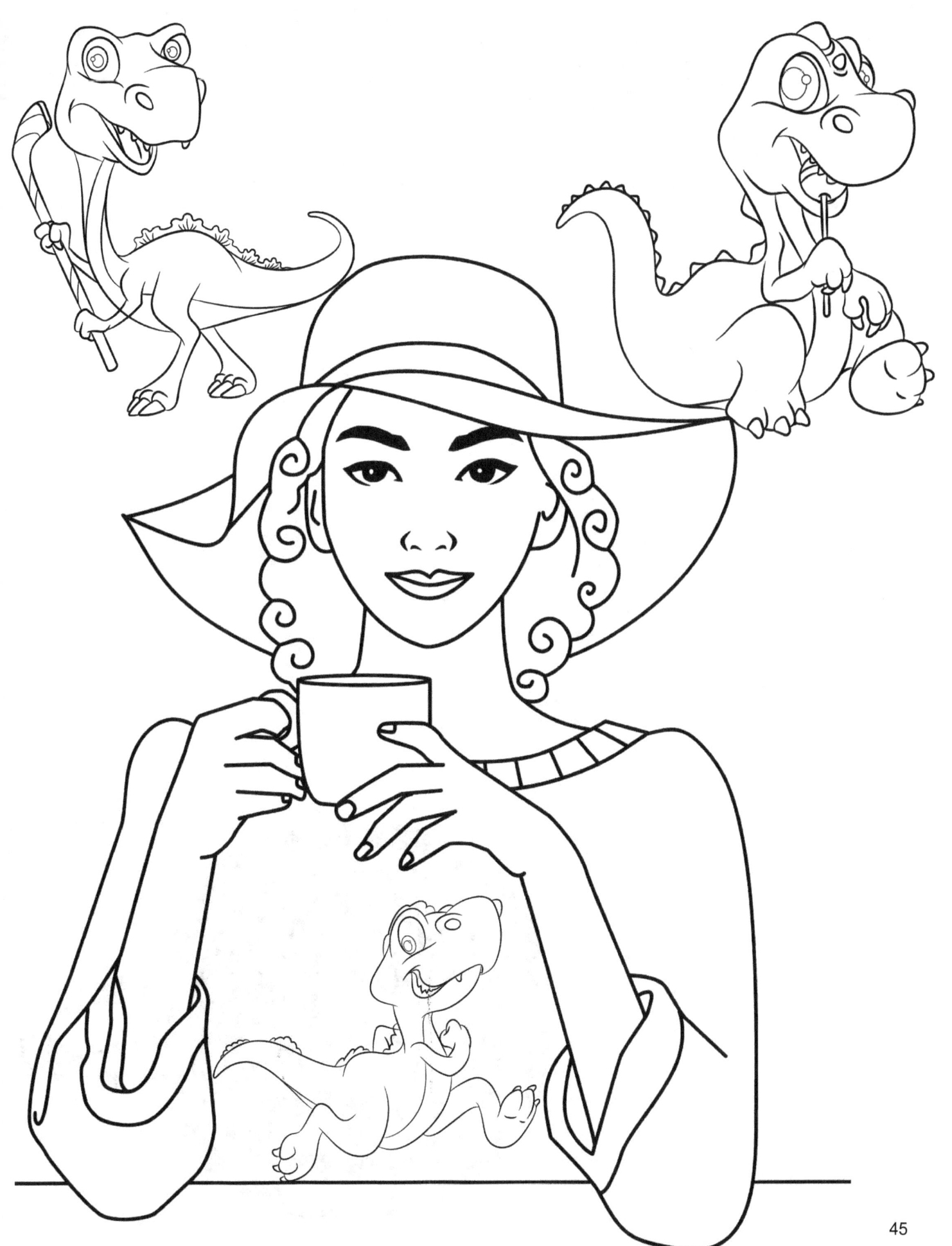

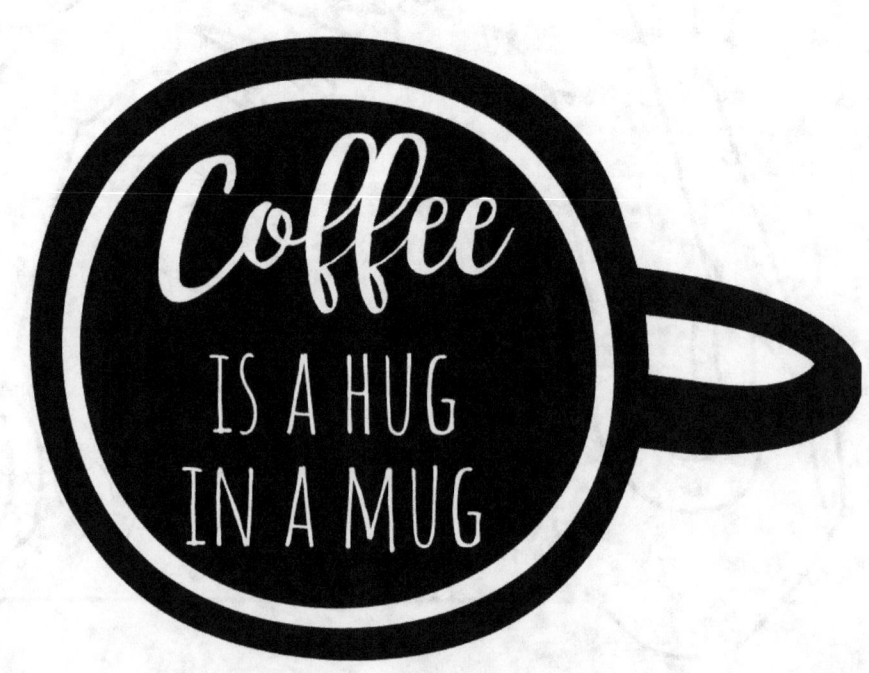

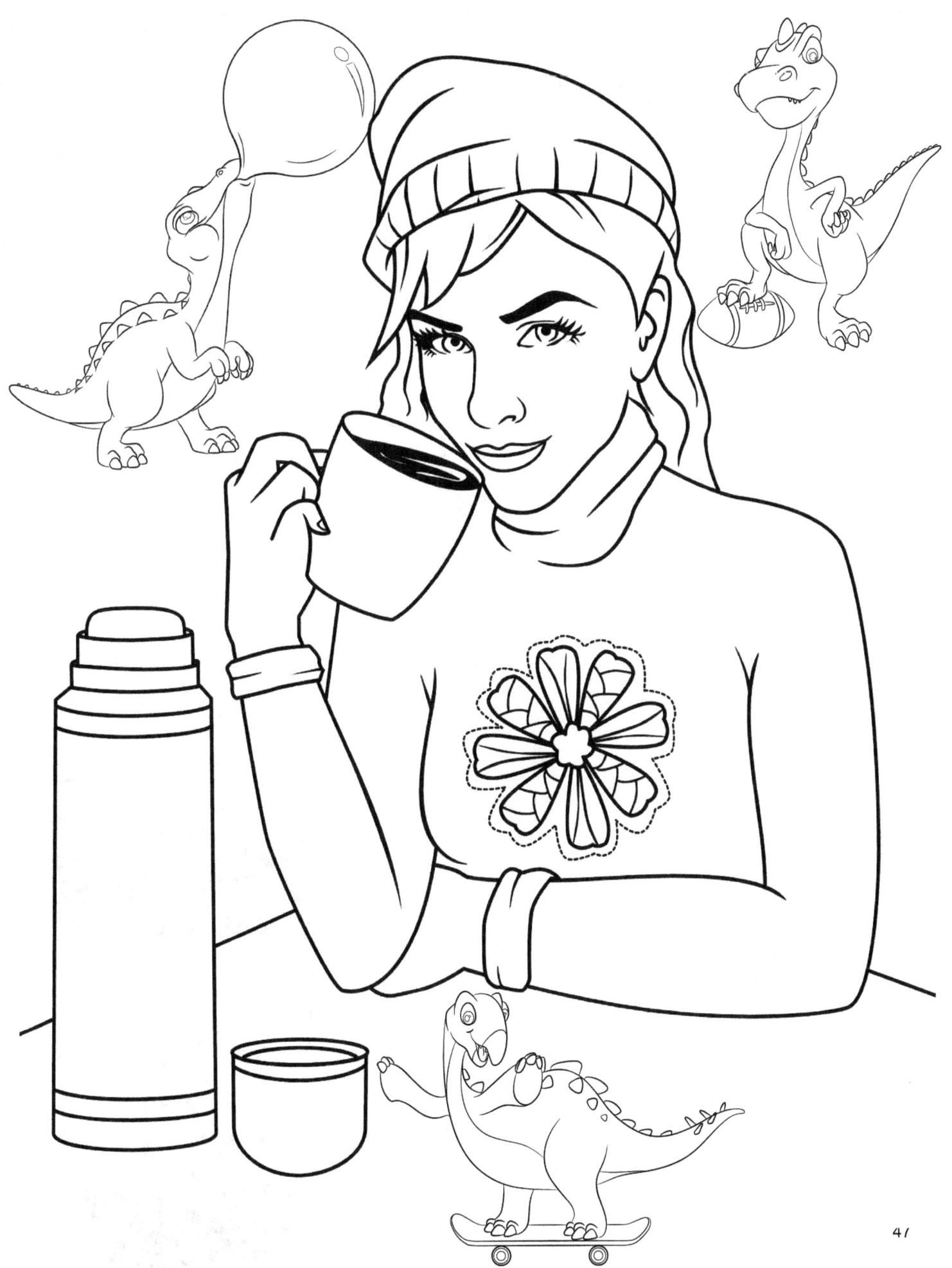

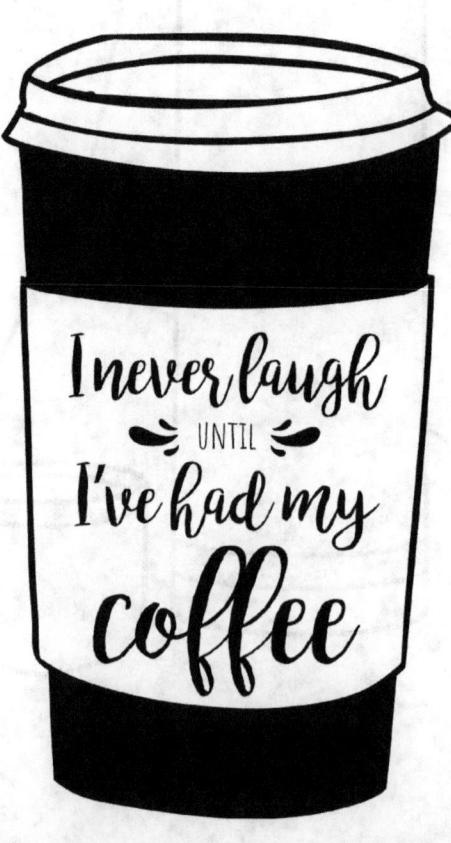

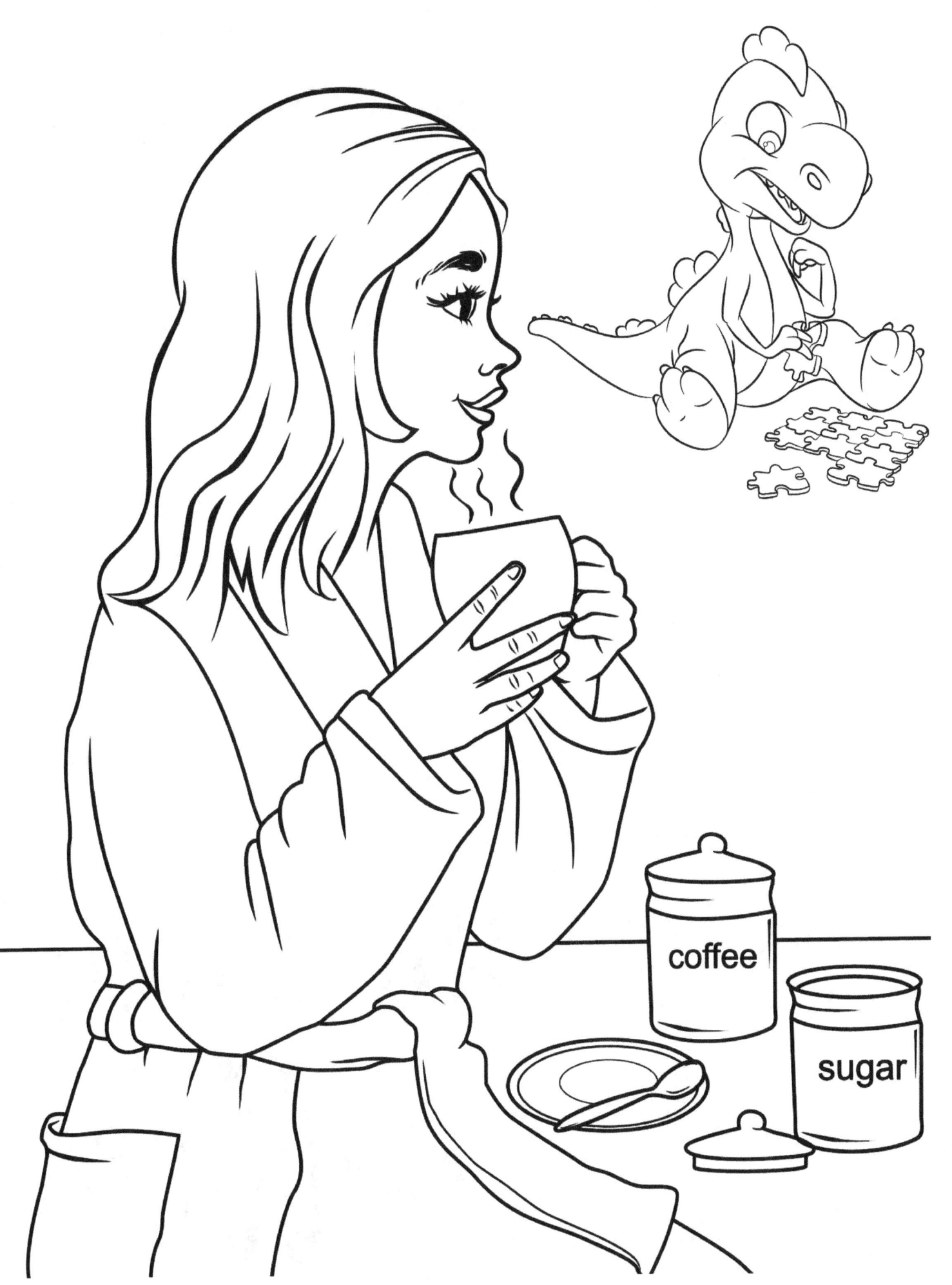

Humanity RUNS ON coffee

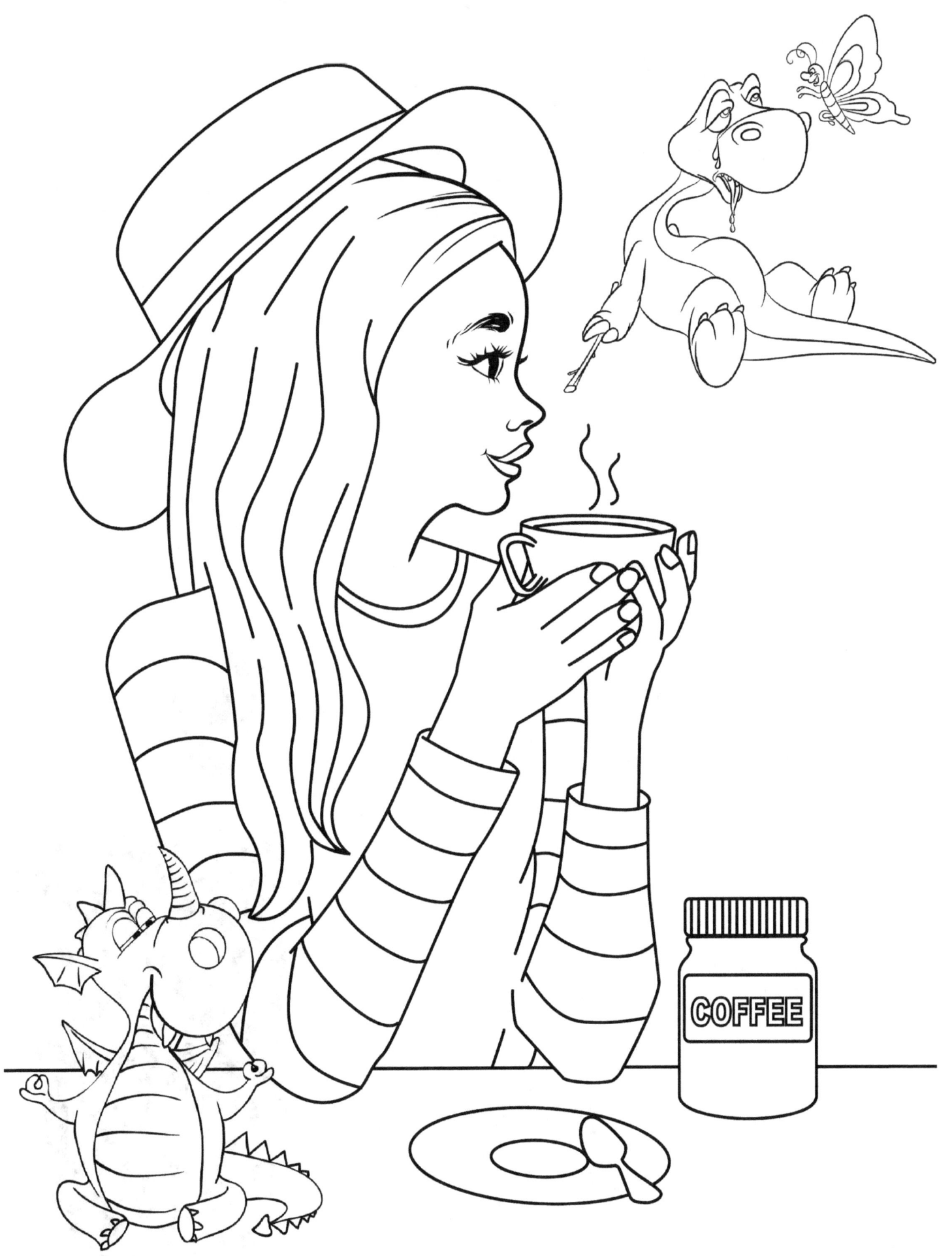

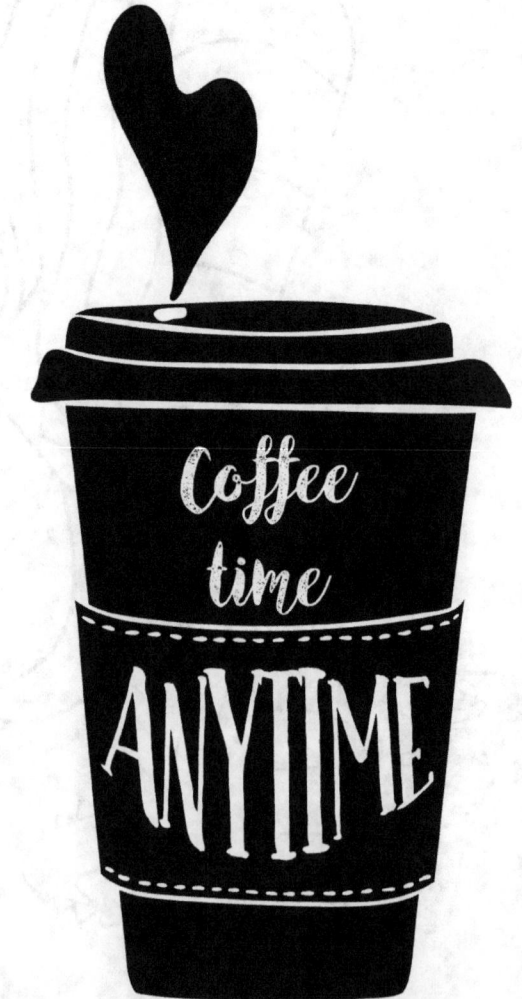

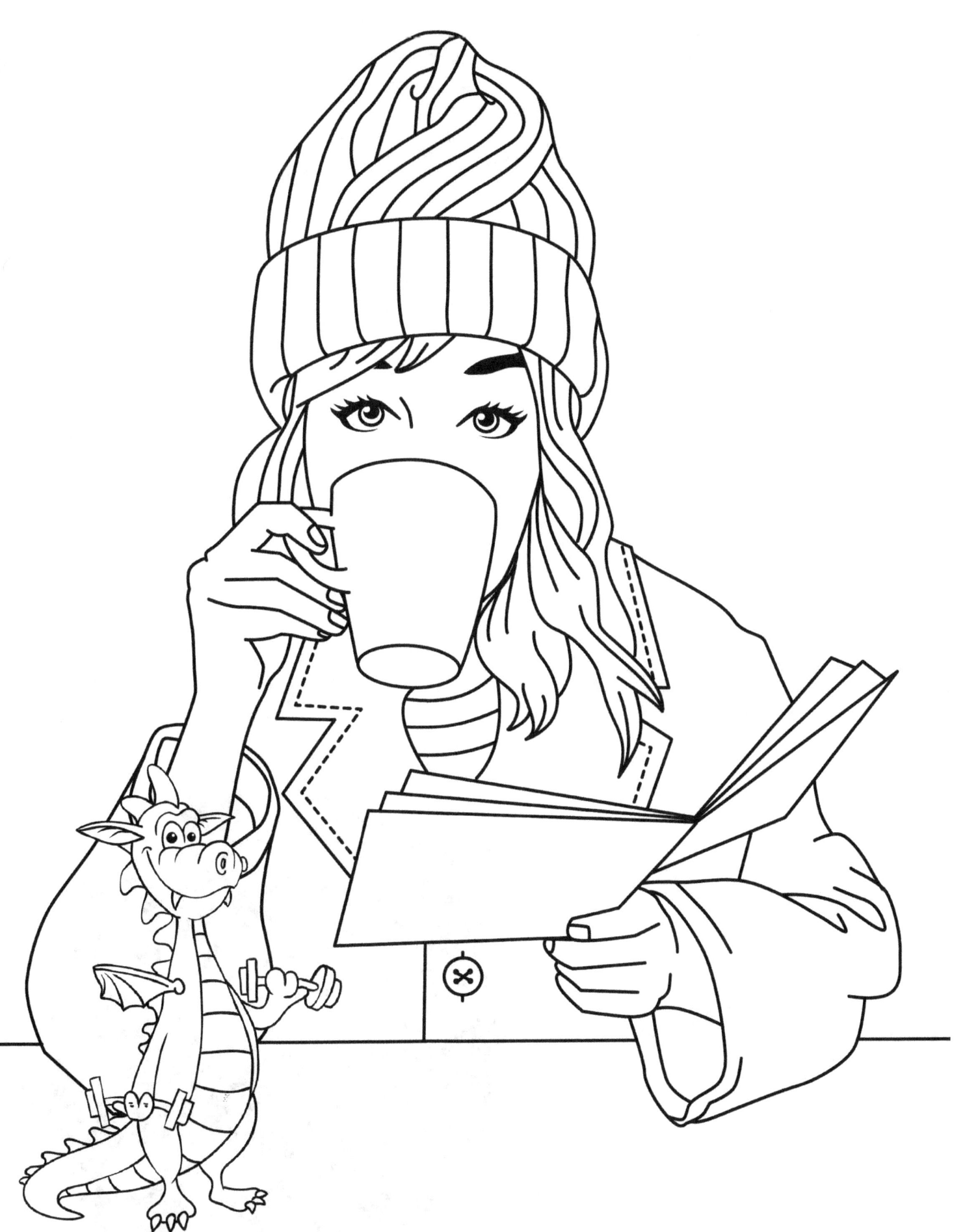

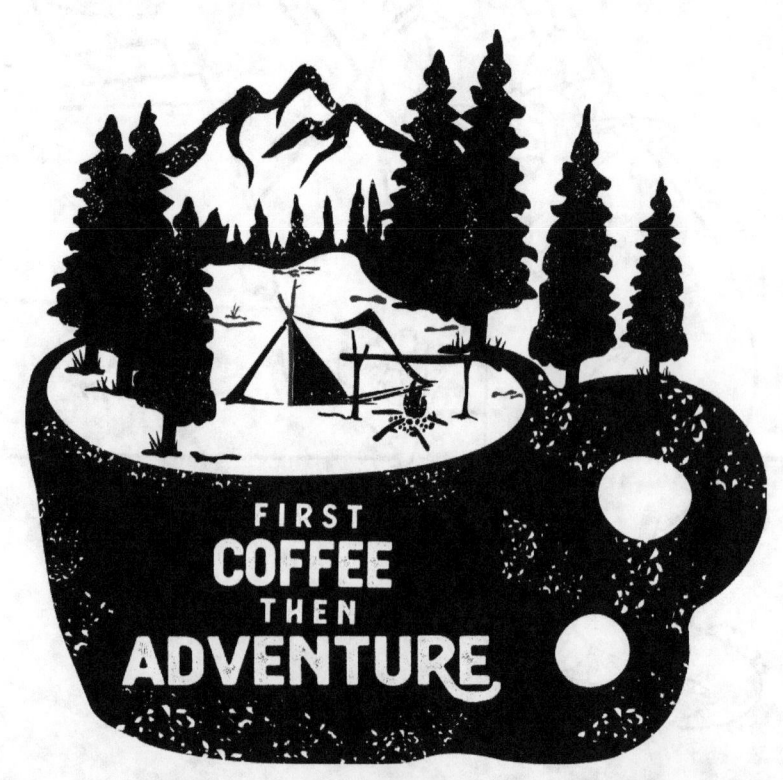

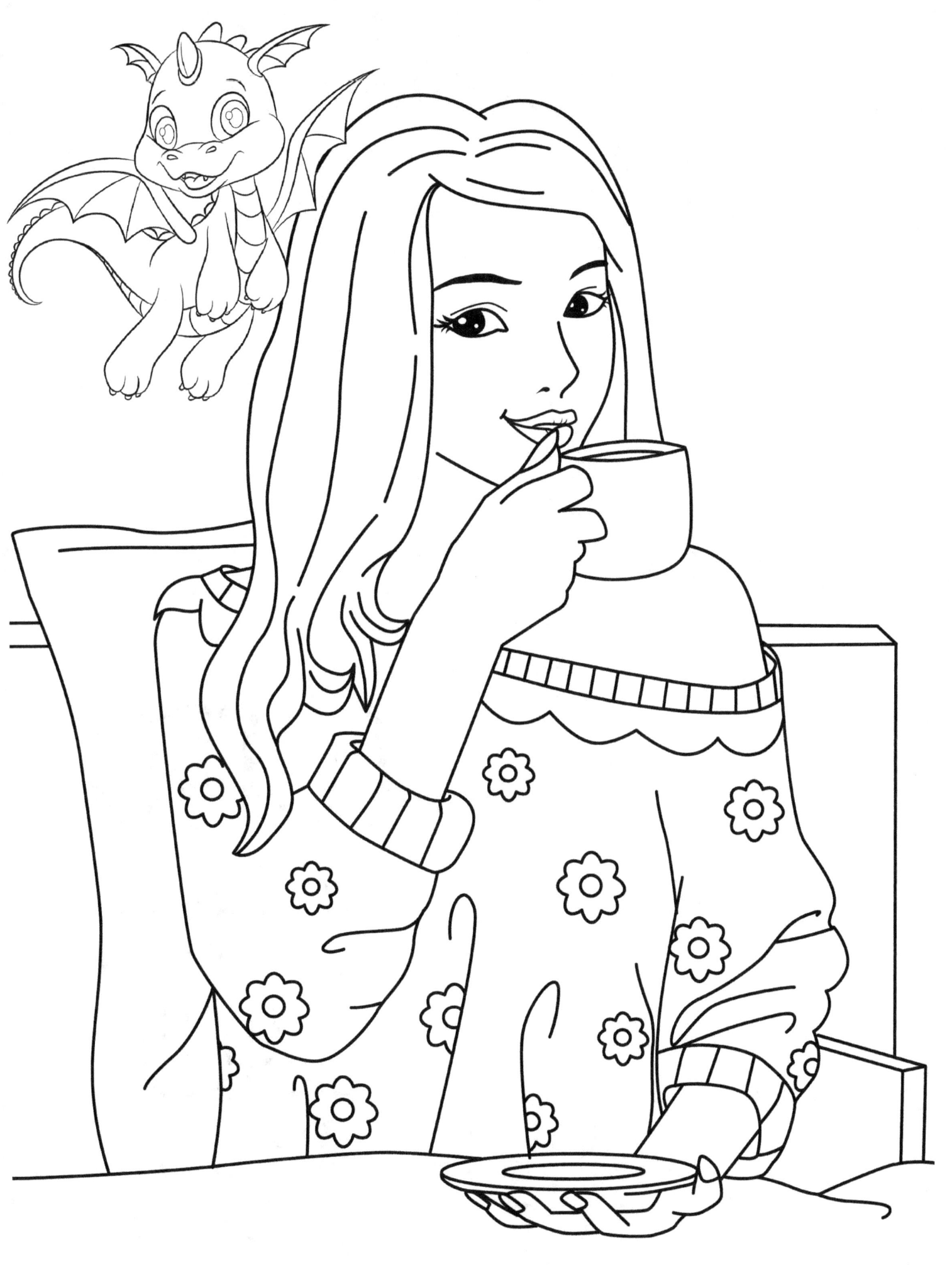

COFFEE...
because
it's too
early
for
BEER

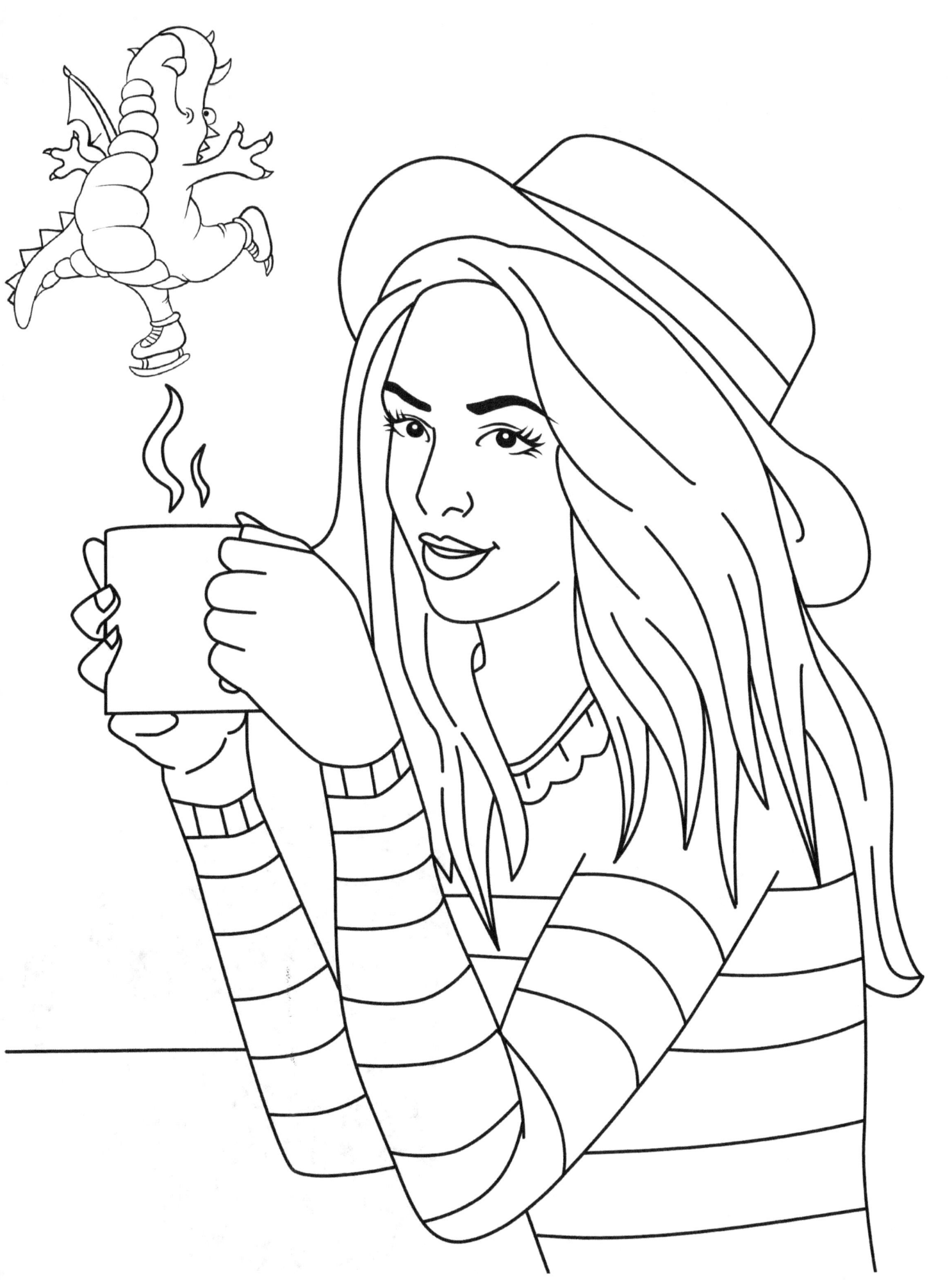

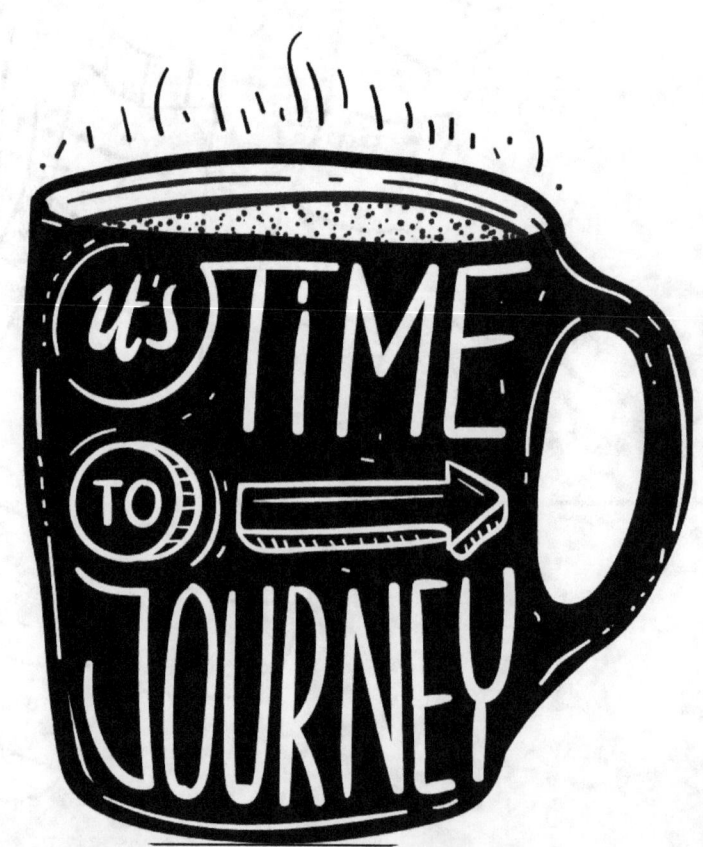

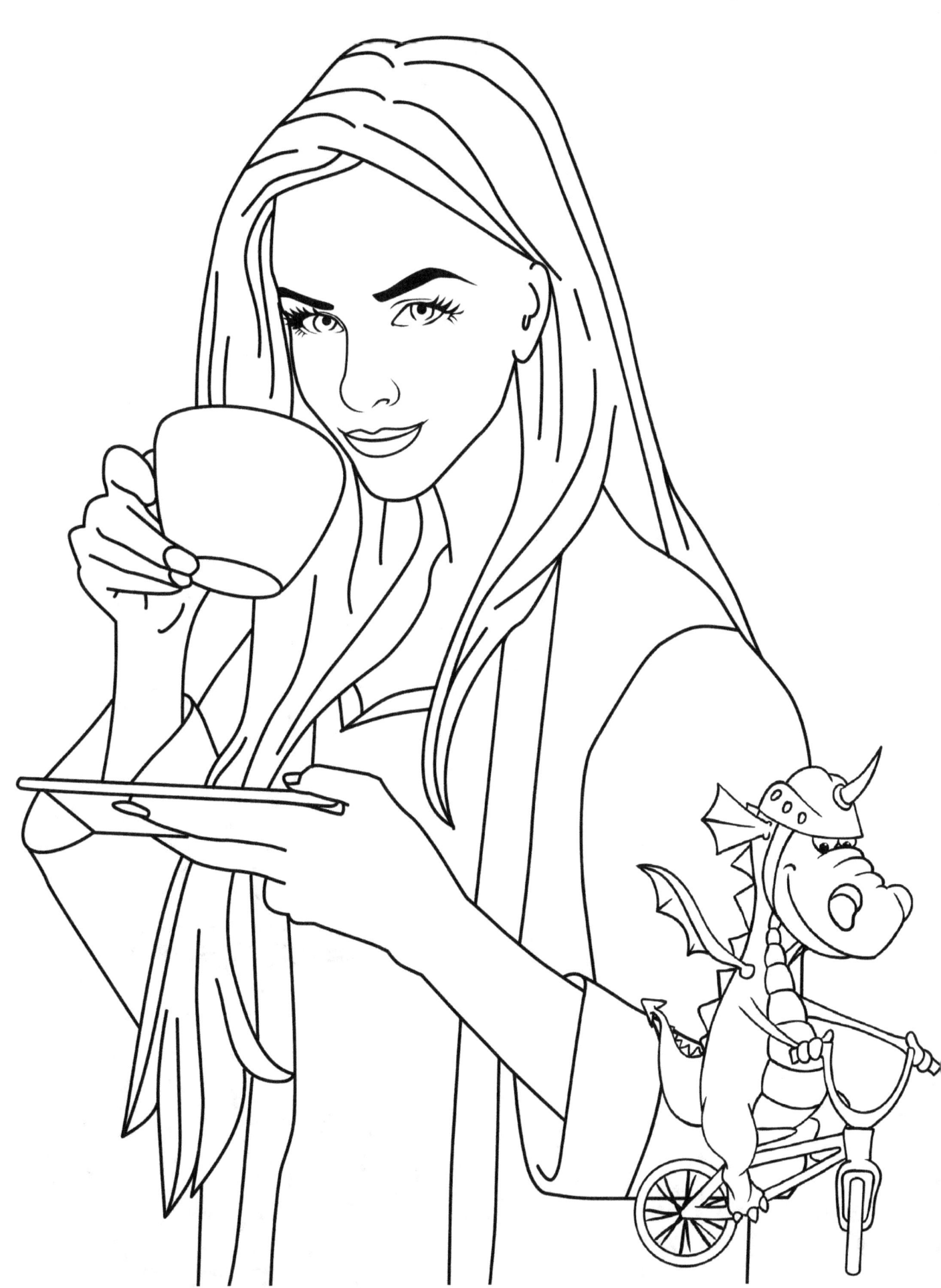

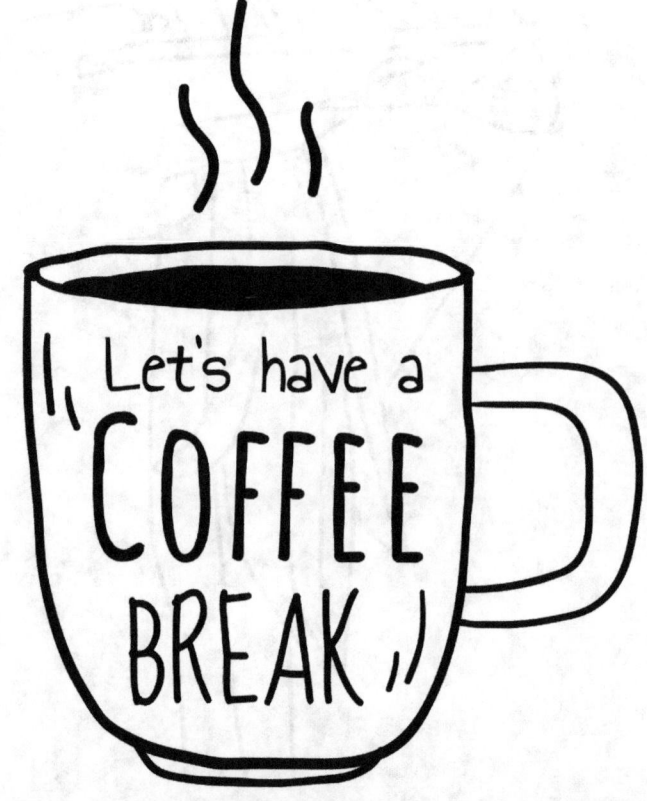

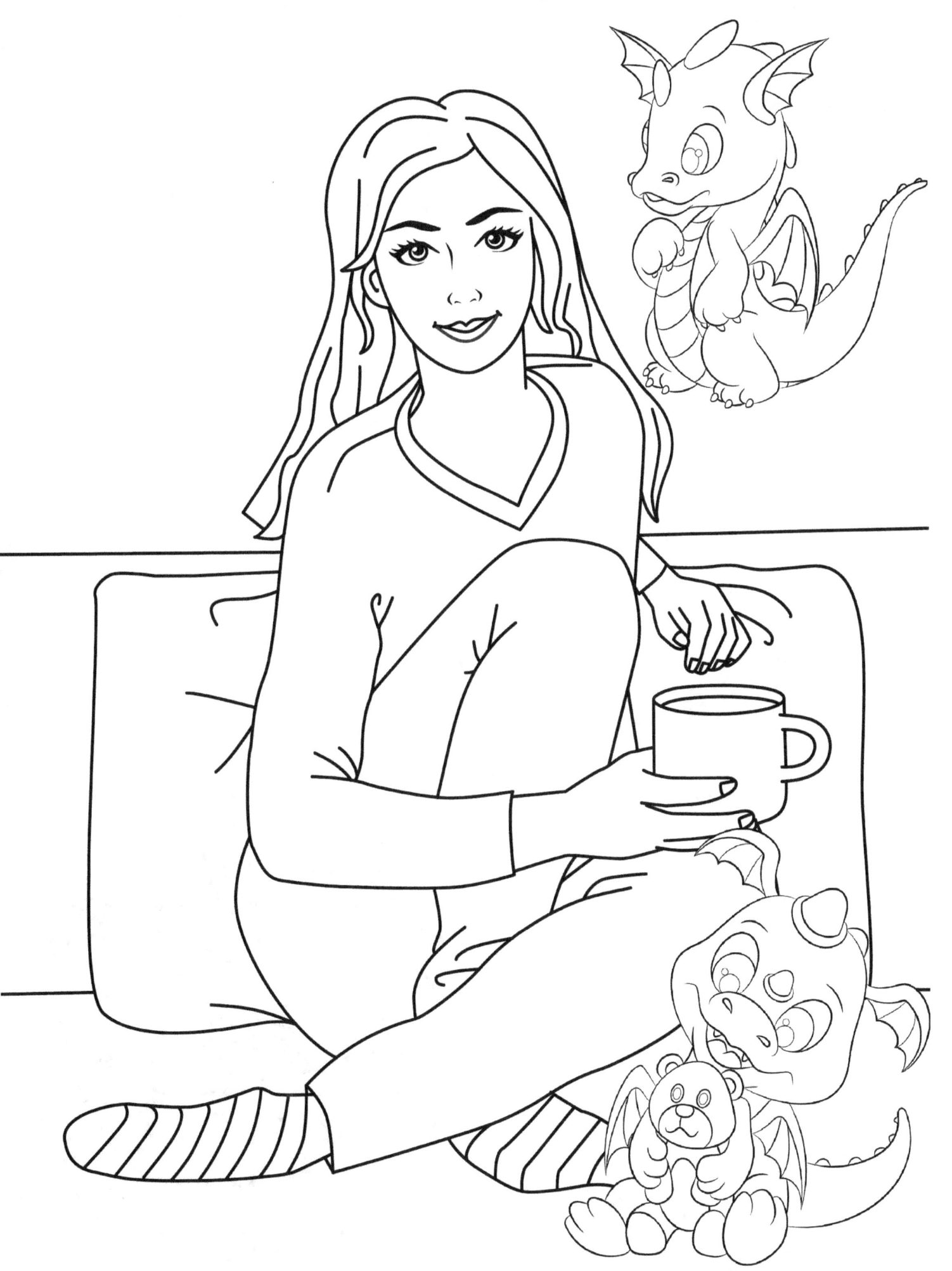

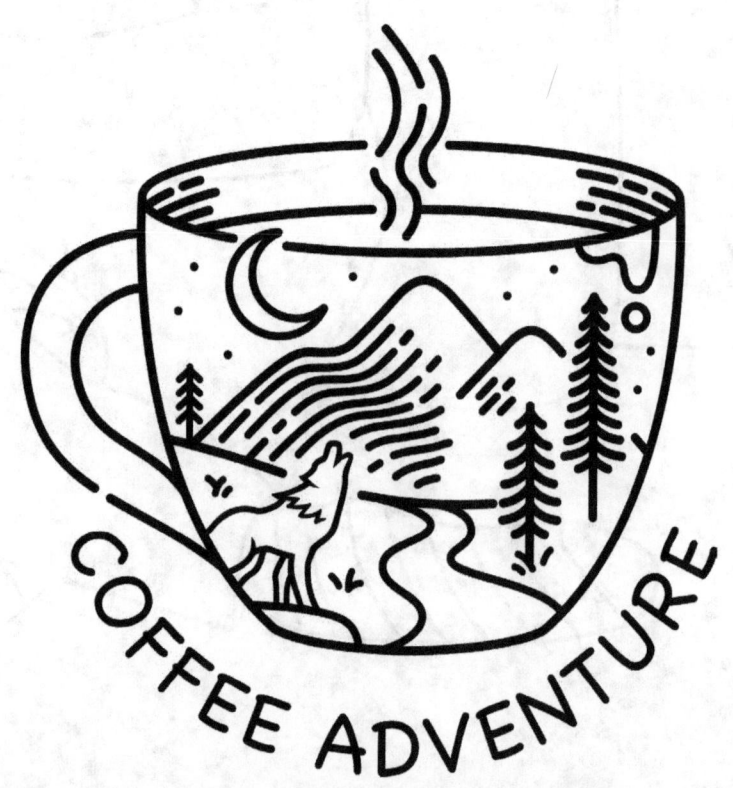

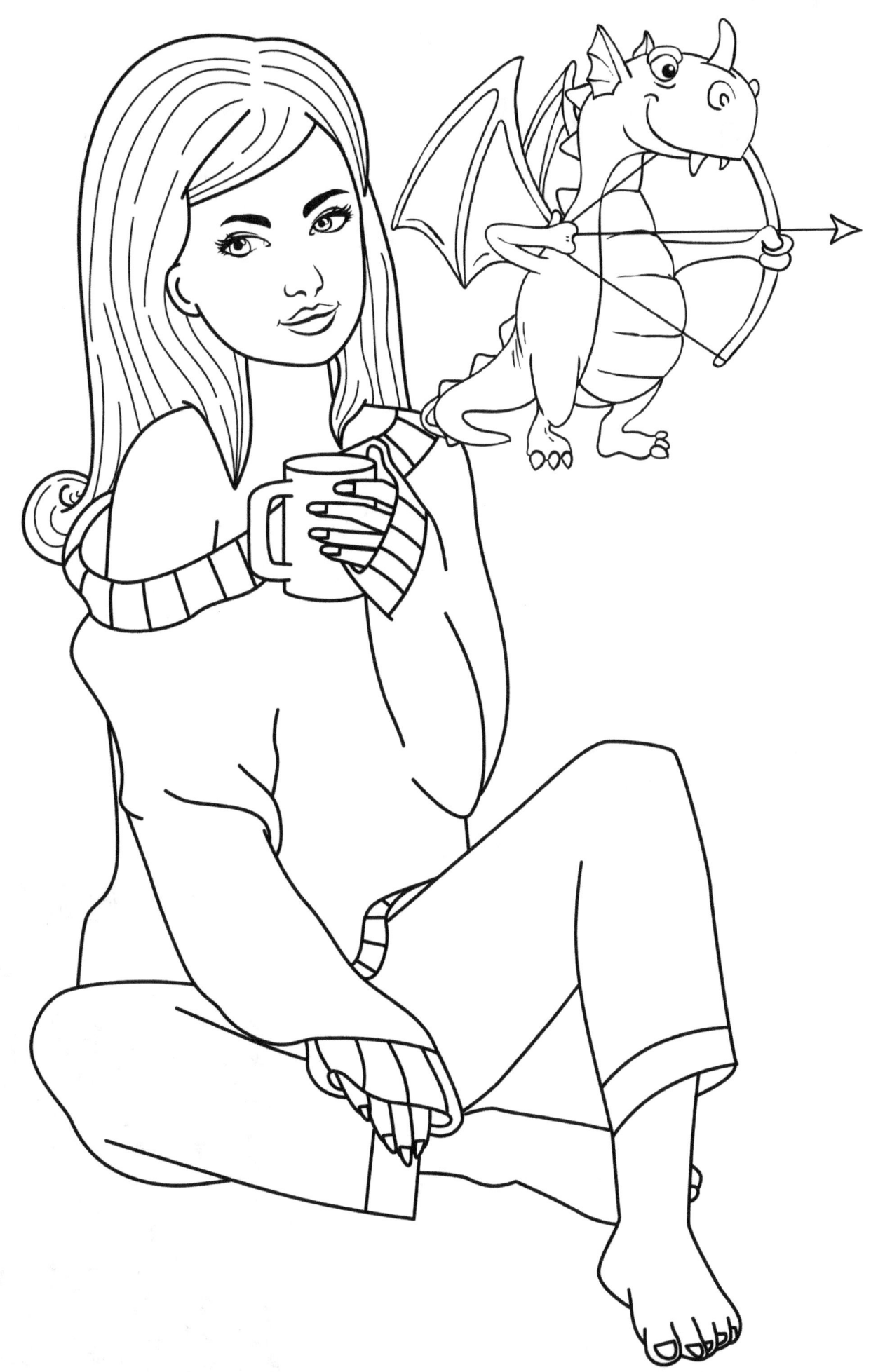

I MUST GET UP MY COFFEE NEEDS ME

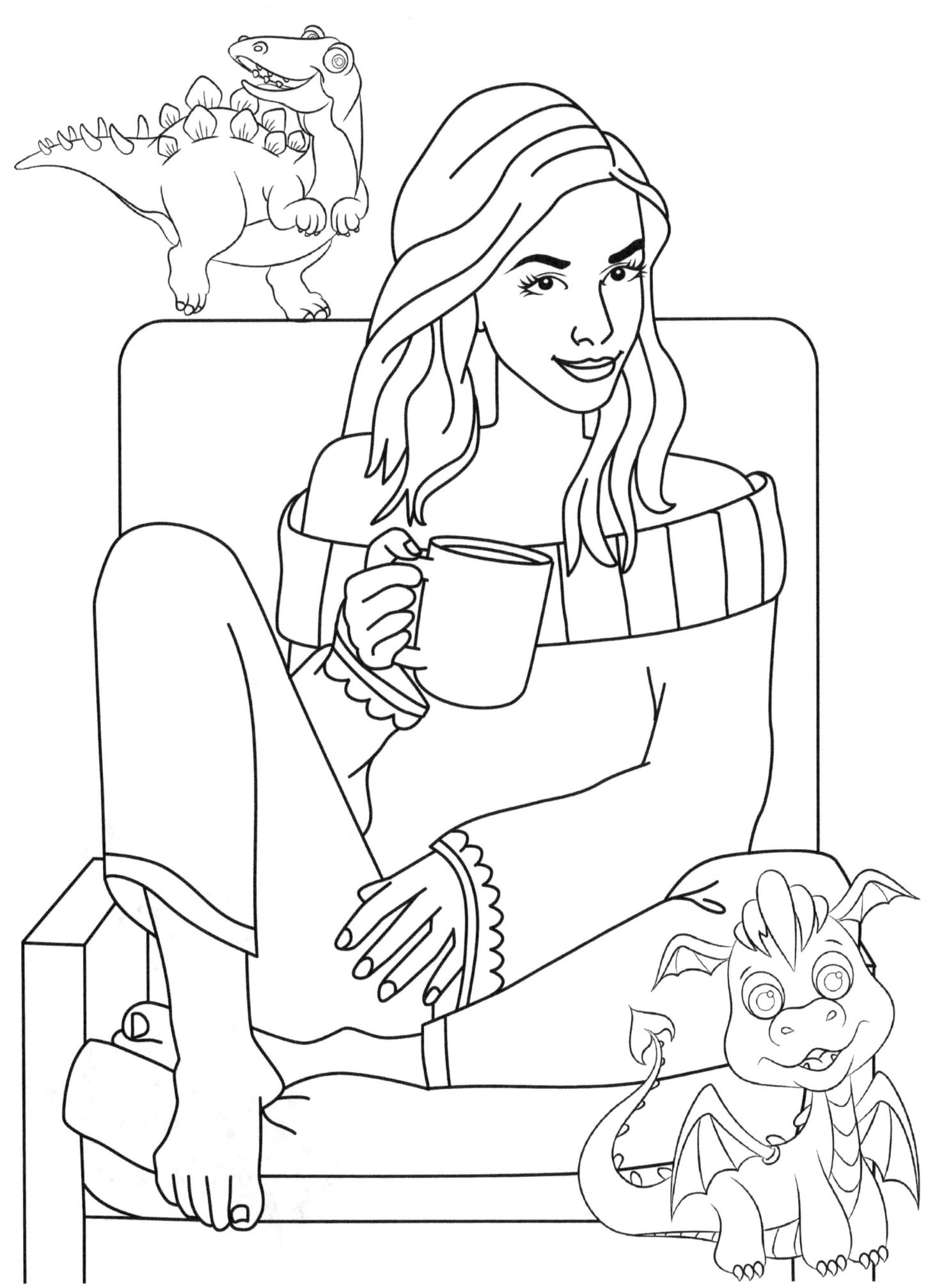

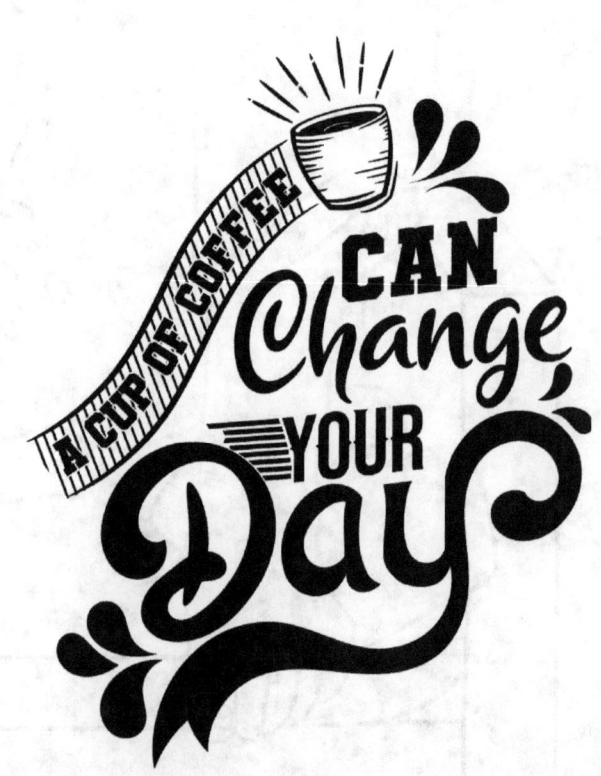

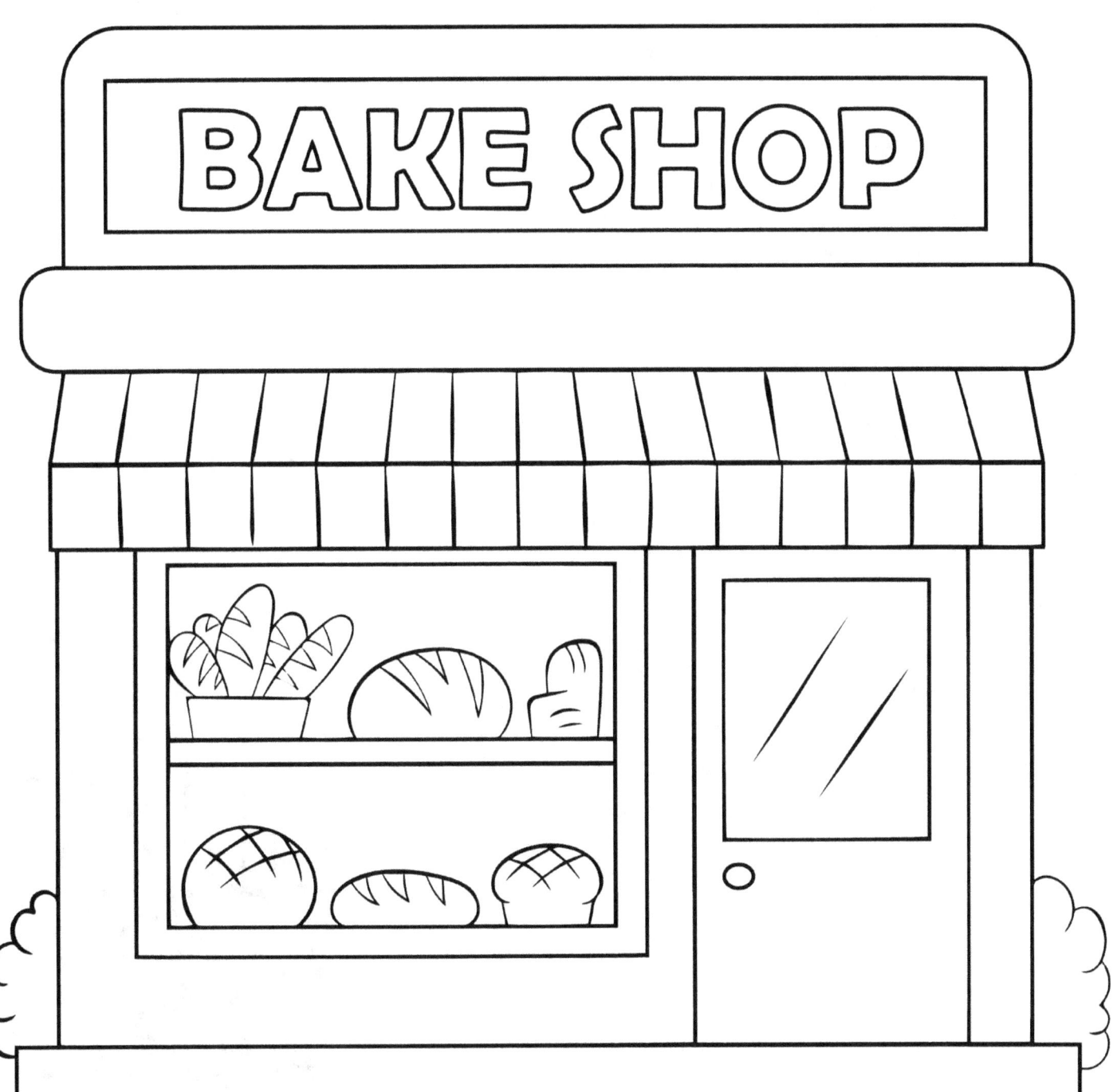

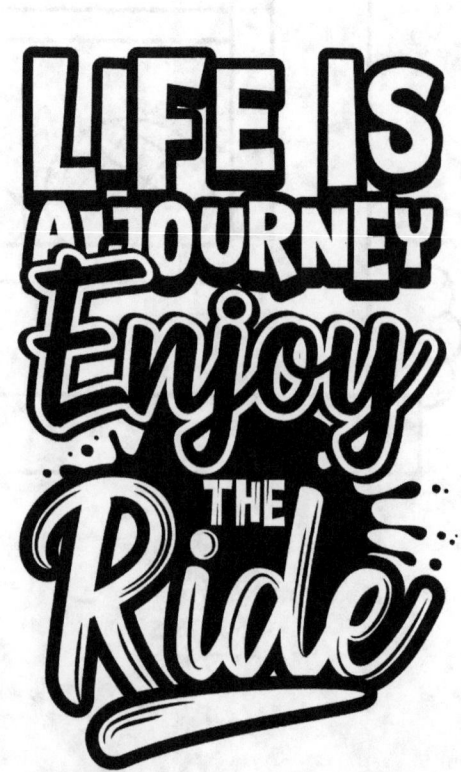

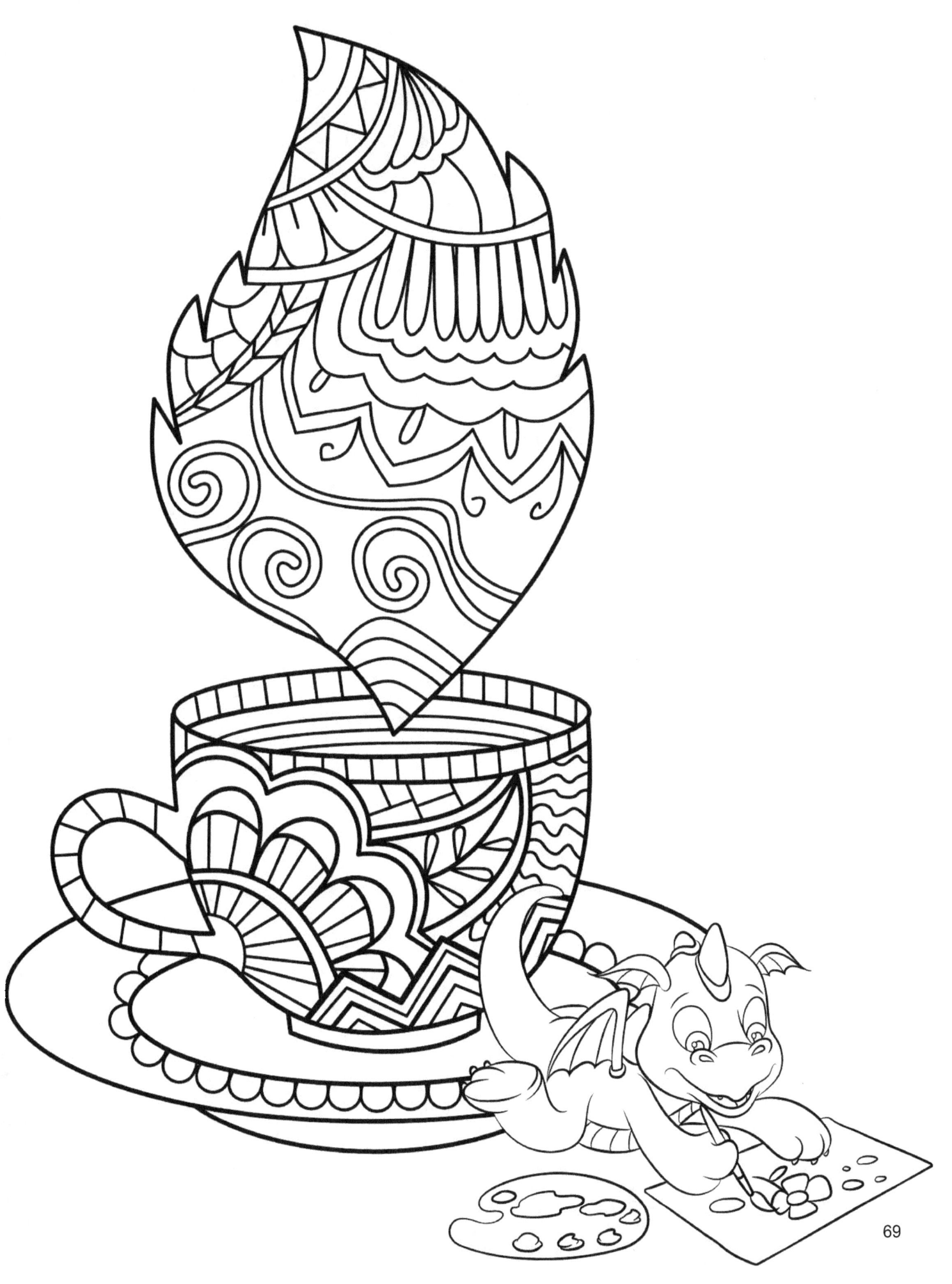

www.ingramcontent.com/pod-product-compliance
Lightning Source LLC
Chambersburg PA
CBHW060438220526

45465CB00008B/3188